The Bank Manager's Handbook:

A Guide to Branch Management

P. A. ELLIOTT

WOODHEAD-FAULKNER · CAMBRIDGE

Published by Woodhead-Faulkner Ltd
Fitzwilliam House, 32 Trumpington Street,
Cambridge CB2 1QY, England
and
27 South Main Street
Wolfeboro, NH 03894-2069, USA

First published 1987

British Library Cataloguing in Publication Data
Elliott, P. A.
The bank manager's handbook:
a guide to branch management.
1. Bank management
I. Title
332.1′068 HG1615

ISBN 0-85941-342-X
ISBN 0-85941-330-6 Pbk

Designed by Geoff Green
Typeset by Hands Fotoset, Leicester
Printed in Great Britain by Redwood Burn Limited, Trowbridge, Wiltshire

Contents

Preface

There is no doubt that bankers taking up their first managerial appointments have had plenty of opportunity to acquire a sound technical knowledge. However, when it comes to the practical art of management, there is remarkably little training available to inform a banker about the things he should expect in his first year or so of management, about the practical difficulties he may now encounter with customers and about his whole approach in taking up his appointment. Experience shows that uncertainty as to how to perform in the managerial capacity and a consequent inability to make the transition from clerical to managerial duties can prevent the new manager from reaching his full potential.

Equally, the failure to make successful relationships with customers can prove a real stumbling block. The ideal situation is one where customers feel they have a bank manager who understands their point of view, who can talk in language comprehensible to them and who gives sound reasons when describing the limits within which the bank can help them. Unfortunately, such a situation is not as common as it should be.

In writing this book I hope to make a contribution towards assisting newly appointed managers through some of the pitfalls of the early years and helping them to achieve a good rapport with their customers. At the same time perhaps I will be able to dispel some of the misconceptions that the student and career banker may have about the demands and realities of branch management. At the very least, I believe that readers of this book will be challenged to consider again how they as banking customers themselves can get the best out of their own bank.

In order to avoid using both the masculine and feminine form on each occasion where it is necessary I have, on the whole, stuck to the male form. I recognise that this is an unsatisfactory representation of the banking world today, but felt that, for easy reading, a single form would be more helpful.

I would like to thank Mr Owen Hawkes for his idea of the mnemonic used in the book. It conveys what I wanted to say simply and memorably. My particular thanks are also due to my wife for her assistance in matters of composition and layout.

Finally, it should be pointed out that all the individuals and companies referred to in the text are entirely fictitious.

Peter Elliott
November 1986

Introduction

Banking is an art and not a science

Whilst the science of banking may be described as the firm financial discipline within which any banker needs to operate, the art is in having the flair to know when to bend with the wind and when not to give an inch. Once it is recognised that the art of banking lies in an ability to keep a continuous balance between implacability and being able to discern an acceptable banking risk, then a valuable lesson has been learnt. Sometimes bankers reach elevated positions by practising implacability in every situation – sticking to 'the rule book' – but banks and their branches are usually more profitably built by people capable of identifying potentially worthwhile customers and going along with them, after a sound assessment of possible hazards ahead. Those who are implacable rarely build anything.

This book is divided into three parts. The first deals with the foundations of management. It follows a newly appointed manager into his first branch and picks up his career in the weeks immediately after his formal appointment, taking him through the matters which ought to be occupying his mind prior to and after arriving at this branch. It illustrates that, quite apart from getting down to the immediate daily problems, there are many things which need consideration in taking long-term stock of the business for which the manager will be responsible. The emphasis here is placed on the personal qualities and attitudes that will be required if the new appointee is to become a successful professional banker.

Part One also looks at the relationship between the manager and head office, which is usually expected to evolve satisfactorily without specific attention. In reality experience shows that lack of attention to this sensitive area is among the main reasons for failure to reach high performance levels. A good relationship cannot be assumed and must nearly always be worked at.

The second part of the book concerns the borrowing customer – his needs, expectations, the manner in which he ought to be assessed – as well as providing guidance on the procedures necessary to maintain credit control and a clean lending book. There are sections showing a manager how to avoid the pitfalls of fraud and the like. The third part of the book deals with various aspects of general branch management. This is a wide field to cover and emphasis is therefore given to those areas which seem to have given rise to the greatest number of problems over the years.

Throughout the book a simplified system of bank control has been used and is shown in the figure which follows below.

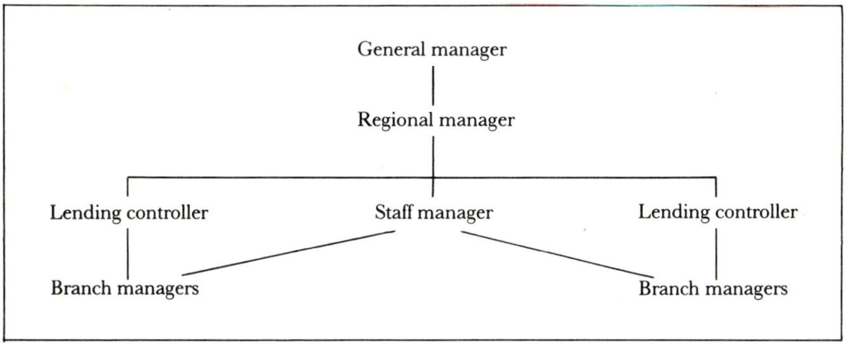

The nomenclature of clearing banks varies. For the purposes of this book the term 'lending controller' has been used to describe the function of supervising lending activity through a head office controller who may be looking after some thirty branches. It is assumed that it is to him that the manager generally refers all his problems, be they lending, property, legal or otherwise. The term 'second-in-command' has been used for the officer who is in charge of the branch during the manager's absence and who is normally engaged in supervising the flow of work through the branch and ensuring that the bank's regulations are kept.

In the second half of the 1980s there have been great changes in the structure of the branch networks of clearing banks. Whilst the old order still remains in many branches, others may no longer, for example, handle corporate accounts; these are now dealt with by a team of lending managers in a local branch or office. The duties of these corporate managers will vary: some will be solely concerned with lending and others with lending plus responsibility for the general welfare of several branches where there are administration managers in charge of the daily business. Although the needs of customers have not on the whole changed greatly, bankers participating in the new order may take up their appointments with a different mix of duties from those of the past. None the less, the foundations and principles of branch management do not change. Those starting in a different situation to that described in this book should easily be able to adapt the information provided to fit their particular role.

PART ONE

Foundations of branch management

CHAPTER 1

In anticipation of branch management

'Time spent on reconnaissance is seldom wasted'
Officers' Training Corps Manual, (1938)

The new manager of the Millchester branch of Barretts Bank is thirty-four years old. It is his first managerial appointment and customers are saying 'Isn't he young – is he experienced enough? Will he be as understanding as the last one was? Presumably the bank knows what it is doing – better give him a chance.'

The banking profession is one in which personality can play a strong part – as shown in the number of customers who follow bank managers from branch to branch when the managers are promoted. However, when a bank manager moves on the main body of customers have to adapt to the new incumbent, as do the bank employees themselves. Unless the previous manager has been a disaster, the advent of the new person will not be particularly good news to the customers. They, like the new manager, are going to have to establish a rapport all over again, and this takes time. As soon as the news of the appointment is out, even as our new manager is receiving the congratulations of family and friends, customers heavily involved in the branch to which he is moving, along with the staff of the branch, are watching the situation closely.

The new manager's first interview with each of his customers sows the seeds of a working relationship, but it will probably take two or three meetings before both sides understand each other and accord each other mutual respect. It could take as much as a year before a new manager feels he has fully settled into his branch, maybe two years in the larger branches.

The first branch appointment is perhaps the most crucial stage of a manager's career. The moment he steps over the threshold on his first morning he must start actively running the branch. His responsibilities to bank and customer begin then, not at some future, unspecified time of his choosing – and he must be prepared for them. Naturally, he may have a little stage fright about it all, but if his management is to succeed it must start straight away.

As the salary reflects, a first managerial appointment is akin to being promoted from the non-commissioned ranks in the army to the level of officer. If the new manager lays down good foundations, he will be able to build a solid career upon them and achieve the strong, quiet confidence which is the hallmark of the professional.

CAUSES FOR CONFIDENCE

Before considering some basic principles for the manager's new life, we need to look at his background. Nowadays, a manager should come to his new appointment well educated and trained for his role. He will probably have become an Associate of The Institute of Bankers by examination prior to leaving the bank's clerical ranks. There is no room in banking today for unqualified personnel at managerial level, whatever the case was in the past. The average business customer expects professionalism from his bank and indeed it is the quality of its professional management that will set one bank apart from another.

After leaving the clerical ranks the manager will probably have had three or four executive posts prior to his latest appointment. These may have been wholly within the branch system or interspersed with periods in a head office or regional office environment. Moreover, he will probably have been in banking for at least ten years and will have attended a number of training courses. His experience will include having been subject to senior staff and having controlled staff himself as his seniority grew. He will have been involved in making administrative and lending decisions and, if he has been alert, will have picked up a great deal from working with the people responsible for taking decisions in day-to-day banking situations. Normally he will also have had plenty of direct contact with customers.

The senior management of Barretts Bank have selected him from a number of candidates as being the best person available at the time to fit into and to carry out the role of manager at Millchester branch. He can take heart from the fact that the management, who are responsible for filling all the bank's managerial vacancies and making a profit, reckon he is the best 'horse for the course'. He should, therefore, be starting the job quietly confident. However, whether he has the self-assurance essential for this job will partly depend on the amount of effort the bank has already put into building that confidence (see Chapter 3 under 'The managerial appointment interview'). A degree of nervous anticipation prior to taking over the branch is natural and is certainly much better than being overconfident. The bank would not have appointed a manager who overtly lacked confidence in his ability to meet the demands of his new job. But nobody has been really tested until they have held sole responsibility for a business: people may crumple under such responsibility or they may blossom.

However, those unduly lacking in confidence should remember how far they have come. They have passed their Institute of Bankers' examinations and have got out ahead of the pack and onto the first rung of the ladder. The personnel manager has, from a background of considerable experience, endorsed the new manager's appointment – presumably on the basis of a good staff report. If he is still worried it may be about the customers – without whom, it has been said, there would be no problems. But there will be sufficient time to learn how to cope with them and the bank recognises that it takes a while to find one's feet. Customers probably appreciate this too and it would be unusual for them to be obstructive over affairs which concern their financial well-being. However, they will expect the new manager to be decisive, to speak with common sense and to give reasons for decisions made.

BASIC PRINCIPLES FOR RUNNING A BRANCH

There are a number of nettles to be grasped in the first year of management. The problem of establishing one's reputation is one of them. One should not be hesitant about stating the bank's case. For instance after listening to Mr Perkins asking for a loan for a new car which he cannot afford and suspecting that perhaps he and his wife are simply trying to keep up with the Joneses, the manager should say nothing less forthright than 'No, Mr Perkins, I cannot lend you the money for the car. We have both explored how you can afford to repay a loan and have proved that your salary is completely committed already. If you have the loan, the bank will finish up by pressing you for the instalments and you would have to sell the car. That means unnecessary problems for both of us'. It is part and parcel of a manager's life to have to decline borrowing proposals and the sooner he learns to distinguish the salient facts in a situation the better. (Chapter 4, 'The borrowing customer – general considerations', describes what happens when a manager cannot say 'no'.) Once the new manager has learned to turn a few proposals down, having provided good reasons for so doing, his confidence will grow. The thought of a difficult interview is often more worrying than the interview itself – particularly for the young manager on the threshold of his first branch.

Impartiality

The need for impartiality is obviously a major requirement in bankers. The bank must show no personal preferences – be they political, racial, religious or social. All customers providing they are honest are of value to a bank: credit balances are the life blood of banking.

This need for strict impartiality can, however, give a bank problems at times. For example, a bank holding the account of a trade union engaged in an unpopular strike may well have customers complaining about their bank retaining such a customer and about normal banking services being provided to the union – including, perhaps, the service of short-term lending to fund strike pay, pending the sale of securities. A bank could lose business from those holding strong views on the subject. Nevertheless, banks and their managers must continue to maintain an unbiased approach to all honest customers. Any deviation from such a policy could lead to reduced confidence in a bank or particular bank branches. The customer's confidence in a bank can take a long time to establish but can be lost overnight – so care needs to be taken to retain it at all times. The need for impartiality extends throughout banking business into all aspects of daily routine. The new manager must be aware at the outset that he must have no favourites so far as business dealings are concerned, although he will undoubtedly get on better with some customers than others.

Dishonest customers are anathema to a bank manager. Sometimes dishonesty can be discerned by the bank in the conduct of an account; at other times it will become known from outside sources such as newspaper reports. Clearly, in this context, the need for care when allowing accounts to be opened is vital. Nevertheless, from time to time it is impossible to avoid such customers and the bank ends up with one on its books. The account must be closed as soon as possible, though proper notice must be given – in accordance with banking law and practice (Joachimson *v.* Swiss Bank Corporation 1921). Failure by a manager to act firmly can often lead to the bank losing money at some future date. Once again, a bank cannot be seen to have dealings with such persons as this too can lead to a loss of public confidence in it. (One only has to see how concerned a bank's head office becomes if its name is reported in a criminal case where the defendant, one of its customers, is convicted, to realise the sensitivity of the issue.)

Charges

The manager's prime task is to make profits for his bank and must therefore negotiate the best possible terms for the bank. This means he should set out to make the same charges for similar transactions across the whole spectrum of his customer base and not favour one customer with lower charges than others – unless there are good business reasons for so doing. Rates of interest and commission charges are discussed by customers outside the bank and the manager who acts in a biased way can damage his future business prospects.

There are two remaining areas of business in which the manager should have sound principles established at the outset – lending and customer relationships.

Lending

The daily payment of cheques and negotiations with customers for borrowing facilities will dominate the life of the bank manager. The situation in different branches does vary but it is not uncommon for him to have four or five lending interviews each day and he will need to devote a fair time to the payment of cheques presented in the clearing. There is a long history in banking of managers being removed from office for failing to perform their lending activities satisfactorily – bankers who were often conscientious and loyal to their bank, but who ultimately failed to control their lending effectively. The reasons for such failure include the reluctance to say 'no', lack of basic lending knowledge, faulty perception, inability to ask the right questions, gullibility (falling for plausible stories without establishing the true facts), neglecting to ask for or to take security when necessary, and an inadequate response to early signs of weakness in the case of existing advances. No doubt the chief inspector's department of any clearing bank could add to this list but it is sufficient here to indicate the general problems which can arise when managers are put to the test in lending a bank's money. (Methods which can be employed to avoid such disasters are discussed in Chapter 4.)

Customer relationships

The banker-customer relationship falls into two parts: the legal, which conditions the actions that both parties may legally take in business with each other, and the physical, which can depend on the manager's 'bedside manner' or 'marketing approach'. At this point we are concerned with the latter part of the relationship – for unless the new manager and his staff get this right a great deal of endeavour can be wasted. No amount of technical competence can overcome the problems arising from managers who are either ineffectual, grumpy, curt, pompous, over-busy or who are unable to relate to the broad spectrum of a bank's account base. It is not unknown to find managers who avoid interviews for fear of making a mistake – a sure sign of self-doubt. Any new manager would be horrified to hear such criticism levelled at him but the pressures of banking life can cause people to change and to lose the common touch. Managers must be aware of this possibility and check it if they realise such a situation is developing.

One of the rewards of banking is the pleasure of doing business daily with people involved in the broadest possible spectrum of occupations on a basis of mutual respect. It may be necessary in the early stages to learn to relate to people from some walks of life where there has previously been no opportunity for contact. A banker newly engaged in management should be aware of the need to adjust his style to that of his customer. Some have a natural ability in this direction, others have to work at it.

If strong personal presentation is important for the manager then it is equally important for his staff. The public rightly expect the same informed civility and service from counter staff as they receive from staff in any other business. One or two off-hand cashiers can easily undo any good the rest of the staff have done.

A good example of the kind of behaviour which should not be allowed to occur took place in a small branch bank one day when a managing director of an engineering company came in to cash an £8,000 wages cheque. As he presented the cheque under the bandit screen with a cheerful 'Good morning' the sole cashier walked away from the counter without a word, left the branch by the front door and came back a few minutes later with a can of soft drink. Upon returning to the counter, the cashier opened the can and drank part of the contents before attempting to deal with the cheque. Flabbergasted, the director told the manager, in good engineering terms, what he thought of such treatment! This may have been a unique case but it seems that the cashier thought it possible to get away with such action: an obvious symptom of weak management. Needless to say, this disrupted an otherwise good relationship – even though the cashier apologised to the director at once.

Banking is a service industry and managers must take positive steps to ensure staff are helpful and attentive to the needs of all customers. For example, a cashier being asked for a foreign currency request form by a customer about to go on holiday might hand one out and then immediately return to bagging-up silver; another cashier in the same situation would take time to assist the customer with the completion of the form – which could present difficulties, although perfectly routine from the bank staff's point of view.

Dealing with queues

Standards of service in a bank must come from the top. Managers must frequently emphasise that only the best will do and should discipline a member of staff when their behaviour is not of a reasonable standard. For example, queues at the counter are an area in which high standards must be maintained as they are a constant source of complaint from customers. In a busy branch, there are times when queues cannot be avoided, particularly over lunch hours – even when staff lunches are staggered between 11.30 and 2.30. However, they can form at other times and this is frequently because cashiers do not ask for assistance soon enough from other cashiers who are working away from the counter (due to an earlier lull in counter activity). However, unless corrected, cashiers will continue to overestimate their ability to deal with a queue and will only ask for help when customers have already been kept waiting for too long. It is the manager's responsibility to point this out for it is a known fact in banking circles that even senior staff fail to take notice of the formation of queues unless they are regularly conditioned to remain alert to them.

The manager cannot, of course, see queues forming when he is in his room and so must make a point of being around the general office regularly. He must be firm will all concerned the first time an unnecessary queue is seen to have formed and he will always need to keep an eye on the situation.

Keeping cool

Managers must be aware of the need to keep their tempers in provoking circumstances and to ensure that staff keep theirs. Customers adopting an unreasonable attitude and passing disparaging remarks about the branch manager or a member of his staff can be a real test of patience. But angry words over the counter will do the bank's image no good whatsoever, especially when there are other customers present in the branch who can overhear the conversation.

Similarly, heated arguments in the manager's room are to be avoided at all costs. Curbing their temper will not only enable managers to think more clearly but will enable them to put the bank's position more effectively once their customer's temper has run its course. When a customer is annoyed it is important to let him finish speaking before putting one's own case. Any interruption whilst the complaint is in full spate is likely to fuel the flames. Where the bank is at fault then the complaining customer must again be heard out before any attempt to apologise is made. The manager should learn to control the conduct of interviews so as to allow the minimum cause for annoyance. He will not always agree with a customer's proposal and his refusal may lead to a strained relationship unless he fully explains his reasons and secures his customer's acceptance. If the customer is smiling at the end of an interview during which his request for an advance has been turned down the manager has achieved a great deal!

SUMMARY

The overall objective of the new manager is to carry out his role displaying a confident, impartial approach and firmly resolved to have a sound lending policy and a high quality of service to customers. Such an attitude will ensure optimum profitability and that he obtains job satisfaction and eventual promotion.

CHAPTER 2

On arrival

'Rome was not built in a day'

Imagine the manager on his first day walking down the banking hall into his office and sitting down for the first time in a manager's chair. Although it will be his first full day's work he will probably already have visited the branch on several occasions. During the time between his formal appointment and his first day he should have met the staff and as many of the customers as time permitted (and as his predecessor thought worthwhile). Hopefully, he will have established a good working relationship with his second-in-command and should have made notes of what he has learnt from his predecessor and head office officials. Apart from that, everything else will be new and a certain amount of initial stocktaking will be essential.

Millchester is a first managerial appointment branch and our new man is the fifth manager in the thirty-three years since the bank opened the branch. (Such a rate of changeover could be average for a branch the size of Millchester.) It is reasonable to suppose, therefore, that such opportunities as there are in Millchester have been fully developed a long time ago. (Otherwise, a succession of managers would have been able to increase the business so that the branch would need a higher grade of management.) As far as general management of the bank is concerned, this branch is one among many branches where opportunities for expansion are limited but where a reasonable profit and an acceptable level of current and deposit account money can be collected for use in the bank's general funding requirement. The limitations that these circumstances appear to impose should not deter the manager from his job. He has been sent to learn his new trade among Millchester's banking public and his head office are expecting that he will not only maintain profits and a high level of service, but will also become an asset to the bank and worthy of promotion.

EFFICIENCY

Whilst the bank does not expect the branch's business to be dramatically increased overnight, it will require a sound performance from the manager as he comes to grips with his branch. This includes ensuring that the administrative regulations and lending policy of the bank are complied with and these tasks should be tackled from the outset.

In banking, as everywhere else, the quality of management will vary from person to person. If his predecessor was good the new manager may need to do little more than thoroughly check all branch systems and practices to ensure the branch is in an orthodox position. On the other hand, the manager may wish to do a great deal to bring the branch up to what he considers to be the right level of operation. This can involve a significant amount of work over and above routine daily tasks. It may well take some time to alter staff attitudes, branch practices, etc., especially if there is a need to alter the composition of the staff or the layout of the premises. Staff will respond well to being firmly and efficiently led if they have experienced such leadership before – and will appreciate such an approach even more if it was lacking in the last manager. The target must be to produce a happy, effective branch which provides good service and has contented customers.

The manager should also ensure that overtime is kept to a minimum. This is important not only from the economic point of view, but also from the staff relations angle. Staff will normally respond better to working unavoidable overtime in a branch they can see being well run than in one which is badly organised.

The reasons for maintaining branch efficiency go well beyond the simple requirement of complying with bank regulations: it is the only way the business can grow. The manager is going to be seeking new business at all times – if only to keep up with the normal loss of accounts by reason of transfer to other branches, death, etc. It is much easier for him to do so if he has an efficient operation behind him because he can then rely on whomever he brings into his branch being well looked after. It will be very embarrassing for a manager who obtains a new company account to find that cheque books have not been ordered, requests by telephone have not been implemented or that the director has been kept waiting unduly long on the phone. Firstly, this manager will have the immediate problem of dealing with the director – who brought the company's account to the bank because he liked the way it seemed to understand his needs but now feels that the bank staff are incompetent; secondly, the manager will be on a knife edge lest the other business he acquires be handled equally inefficiently. News of bad management like this travels quickly outside the bank as well as inside and the manager cannot afford to let such a situation develop. There is no reason for putting up with poor systems or lax staff attitudes, and firm discipline in this area is especially important in situations where it has been tolerated in the past.

DECISION-MAKING

This is a useful point at which to consider decision-making – a difficult area to get just right. There are usually two polarities: the man who can never make up his mind and come to a decision, and the man who makes his decisions so quickly that he does not give himself time to properly consider the situations. Neither extreme is effective in branch banking where many decisions have to be taken daily.

The quantity of correspondence passing over a manager's desk daily is such that, by and large, he only has time to read it once. As soon as the facts of a matter are known a decision must be made and implemented because there is usually plenty more work waiting behind that particular item. Pushing papers aside, although a natural reaction, is a bad practice – not only because it wastes time but also because it encourages further indecision.

In particular, problems over the payment of cheques presented in the clearing require a decisive approach. Every day there will be some held out by the cancellors pending a decision on whether to pay them or to dishonour them. Some managers put off the decision-making until the close of business in case the customer(s) pay in to their accounts but this only serves to delay the office routine further. Generally, all the pertinent circumstances are known about the cheques by the time the clerk brings them to the manager – hopefully before lunch. There is nothing to stop the manager deciding to pay some and to return the rest unless funds are paid in to cover them. Towards the end of the day the manager should always see cheques actually being returned before they are put in the post. This serves as a reminder to the manager in case something has happened during the day to alter his earlier decision and which he has not had a chance to pass on to the staff concerned.

Staff queries need to be dealt with by giving definite instructions as to the action to be taken; where there is room for doubt, the staff member should be made to repeat the manager's instructions to ensure that they are both on the same wavelength.

Although it is important to be aware of the consequences of any decisions taken, managers must avoid looking over their shoulders in reaching a decision. The manager must always act in the light of what is best for the bank in the circumstances. What the customer will say, what the staff will think, even the attitude of a head office need not influence the manager strongly, providing the decision is within his authority to make. Historically, banks have always permitted a good deal of autonomy to their managers – indeed, this is essential for the conduct of good banking. However, with such freedom comes the need for sound, independent judgement and this cannot be achieved satisfactorily if a manager is over-concerned with what others may think.

On some occasions, however, a manager will need to consult his head office, for example, when faced with a situation that is new to him and presenting legal or lending problems beyond his experience. A prime function of the lending controllers who are based at head office is to act in a consultative capacity. Initial discussion of a complicated situation is far better than having to unravel subsequently the results of a wrong decision which has led to a loss of money.

DELEGATION

In today's business environment the average manager will have difficulty in finding time to carry out all his responsibilities on his own. He must therefore delegate to members of his staff, although he will obviously retain ultimate accountability for their actions. However, delegation does not mean abdication of responsibility. The manager who for some reason has become lazy or uninterested may leave virtually the entire running of his branch to his staff. This is a recipe for disaster as successful delegation always depends upon good general supervision of those to whom authority has been given.

Some people never master the art of delegation and even those who are experienced in management may wonder from time to time whether they have got it quite right. Some people fall into the trap of not recognising the need to delegate and can create a work pattern for themselves which they find difficult to maintain with the increasing pressure of their responsibilities. This can lead to a preoccupation with detail which takes the manager away from more important work that would yield greater profit to the bank. The feeling that 'It's quicker to do it myself' may sometimes be justifiable but it can also be an excuse used by people who are instinctively secretive and who fear losing control. Others may lack confidence in the staff or without cause might even fear that other staff will actually do the work better than they would themselves.

There have been innumerable cases where managers have become over-involved in routine branch work to the detriment of their more important duties. It seems as though, having been trained in a clerical capacity up to management level, they are unable to break out of that mould and assume their new role. This can lead to many aspects of business development being neglected whilst the manager carries out the functions of a senior clerk – possibly because such tasks seem easier than those which must be executed at management level. This danger must be recognised and any such tendencies nipped in the bud.

Much of the work in banking requires that a balance be struck between a manager and his staff in order to deal with the daily tasks of banking life. Circumstances will dictate how that balance is to be struck. Decisions about what to delegate will depend on the actual business and level of staff activity. However, as a general statement, all routine matters must be passed down to the staff through the second-in-command, leaving it to the latter to see that the work is carried out and to sign the related correspondence. This might cover, for example, the opening and closing of accounts, night safes, cheque and credit cards, travel and other routine international work (such as mail transfers and bills for collection), statements, cheque books, stopped cheque instructions, stock exchange transactions, safe custody, returned cheques inwards and outwards (except those due to lack of funds), standing orders, direct debits, opening the post (a second-in-command's duty), cancelling and stationery. It can also include negotiations about small lending and personal loans. Interviews and telephone calls in respect of this work should be delegated unless absolutely necessary.

Having delegated, there must be a feed-back system. It is essential to ensure that the second-in-command and the staff report back anything out of the ordinary about customers' activities. The manager must always keep his door open to allow staff to pass on information, and care must be taken not to discourage them from so doing even though someone else may have already reported the matter.

Having delegated, the manager may well be pleasantly surprised by the capabilities of his staff, who will, in turn, be encouraged by being given more responsibility. Delegation will also assist the manager in training his staff and will give him opportunities to assess their abilities (about which he will have to write in their staff reports).

REVIEW OF BORROWING ACCOUNTS

Part of a manager's stocktaking activities on taking over a branch is an initial review of all borrowing accounts to ensure that he is satisfied with the bank's position in each case. It is rare for managers to be entirely satisfied with all the accounts they inherit. Usually, there are some bad or doubtful borrowing accounts and these may be divided into three categories:

1. accounts already reported to the lending controller;
2. accounts which need to be reported to the lending controller but have not been so far;
3. accounts where a potential loss falls within the manager's discretion.

In the case of the first category, the branch will have been in correspondence with its lending controller and a line of action will have been agreed upon and should already have been implemented. However, the manager may come to a considered opinion that there is no hope of recovery or that the current approach could be improved. If so, he must not hesitate to say so.

The second category should be reported as soon as possible with a suggestion about a possible line of action (backed up by sound reasons). If a manager inherits a branch which has an excessive number of accounts in this category, he should not hesitate to report the fact at once. He will be held responsible for all the lending from the time he arrives at the branch and for his own protection should, therefore, ensure that head office are aware of any potentially untoward situations.

The third category also needs a statement outlining the overall situation if there is an undue number of existing accounts. There will usually be an acceptable number requiring attention and a decision has to be made whether to write them off as bad debts or to negotiate a satisfactory repayment scheme.

This borrowing review will be time consuming, but is essential. Its purpose is to help the manager learn about each borrowing customer and to help clear out any dead wood. Until this is done, the manager can be hindered by a legacy of difficulties from a past administration.

His goal must be the freedom of a clean lending book. In order to clear the way for such a situation he may need to interview certain customers about putting their accounts in order and this will in itself generate a good deal of correspondence and related work.

CREDIT CONTROL

Credit control is a prime managerial function. The new manager must therefore make certain from the outset that the arrangements for it are completely satisfactory. Credit control covers all aspects of:

1. the collection and payment of cheques;
2. dealing with uncleared effects;
3. correspondence regarding lending and its follow-up and lending reviews;
4. the taking of security;
5. the daily inspection of computer print-outs showing out-of-order situations;
6. the input to computer of limits, rates of interest and other recorded information, with the proper grouping on computer of connected accounts with set-off where applicable;
7. the procedures for staff to refer cheques drawn in excess of available balances, or in excess of the account limit to the manager for a decision as to payment or dishonour;
8. the system for dishonoured cheques returned to and by the branch;
9. adequate written records being kept of interviews and correspondence affecting arrangements made with each customer;
10. all allied matters such as stopped cheque procedures.

The result of the review must be to ensure that the branch cannot unwittingly pay a cheque or enter into any other liability which could result in a loss. A reasonable system will probably already exist. However, the manager must ensure that he is personally satisfied with the situation because he is ultimately responsible for credit control and that overall responsibility cannot be delegated. Particular attention needs to be paid to the full recording of interviews, telephone calls and correspondence affecting the conduct of accounts. If the manager carries such arrangements in his head, difficulties are bound to occur when members of staff are faced with a problem in his absence or when he simply forgets what has happened. Very few arrangements made with customers need be considered confidential to the manger. It is customary to circulate daily interview notes etc. amongst senior staff, using these notes to instruct staff of any action necessary.

THE SECURITY OF CASH AND PREMISES

This is another stocktaking priority. Normally a new manager will be aware of the requirements of his bank regarding security. In this case, Barretts Bank will undoubtedly have comprehensive instructions for the protection of cash, staff and premises to which the manager must strictly adhere. If the branch thinks it cannot apply all the regulations for any reason then it should obtain a written dispensation from the chief inspector's office. This may well involve a visit by an inspector in order to resolve the problem.

The strong-room, keys and codes

It is essential that bank regulations regarding the prevention of physical loss of valuables kept within the branch are followed. Strict observance of the regulations in this area of work will reduce any possibility of a loss to the absolute minimum. A manager will be heavily criticised if his control of aspects surrounding the strong room, keys, codes and cash is found to be in any way imperfect.

The precise arrangements for control and security of the bank's strong-room are not only confidential but will vary between branches within any bank depending upon the estimated risk, the type of security device installed and the types of strong-room door, etc. It is common practice, however, to forbid anyone to be alone in a strong-room, i.e. dual control invariably operates for all that goes into and comes out of a strong-room.

When the strong-room is opened in the morning the only cash to leave it will be the money contained in the individual tills of each cashier and such additional cash as is estimated that the cashiers may require during the day. The manager and his second-in-command should then check the remaining cash in the strong-room to ensure that the total agrees with the bank's books. A similar check should take place if there is any need to add to or remove cash from this reserve of cash during the day. The reverse procedure will, of course, occur at the close of business with the manager and second-in-command signing for money arising from the cashiers' transactions during the day. The importance of this final check of cash to be left in the strong-room overnight cannot be over-emphasised.

From the security aspect, it is very important that the cash should be locked away as soon as the cashiers have agreed their tills with the day's book-keeping. This may well take place an hour or more before the staff have finished their day's work. It would be quite wrong to leave cash in the counter area during this period when it could be locked away securely in the strong-room.

The contents of the bank's strong-room will include other items besides cash, such as deed boxes belonging to customers, securities held either in safe custody or as security for bank advances and sundry other items which the bank or customer feels should have the protection of the strong-room. When any item is lodged in the strong-room it needs to be taken in under dual control in the same way as cash and two authorised officials must sign for receipt of items in the strong-room. When they are eventually reclaimed they will be signed out of the strong-room so that there is always a written record of items in the strong-room. Obviously any items removed from the strong-room either to await collection by a customer during the course of the day or for inspection by the staff, need to be locked in a secure drawer or cabinet at all times, pending delivery to a customer or their return to the strong-room. The dangers of leaving valuables lying unattended on desks are self-evident and staff who act in this manner must be corrected.

The normal method of maintaining security over areas in which valuables are lodged is by having dual control of the locks on doors and drawers. In this way no one person can gain access to such areas without the assistance of another and both are then equally responsible for the movement of the items inside. The locks may be controlled by keys or codes. It is normal practice for members of staff who have control of one set of keys or codes not to permit another member of staff to handle the keys or to know the code – unless that member of staff is part of a group authorised to handle that particular set of keys or codes.

It is also essential to keep all doors leading off the banking hall into the office section of the branch locked during opening hours. There is a prime security risk whenever the exterior doors of the branch are being opened or closed and consequently considerable care needs to be taken to ensure that security arrangements are enforced at all times. Properly controlling cash, keys and codes outside the strong-room area is of paramount importance. This includes controlling the activities of the cashiers in the counter area.

Strict compliance with bank regulations concerning the premises, the strong-room and cash will virtually eliminate any chance of the branch having a serious loss. It is therefore of the utmost importance that this area of the branch operations be kept under regular managerial review. Any tendency towards slackness must be dealt with firmly.

HOURS OF WORK - INSIDE AND OUTSIDE THE BRANCH

The new manager should ensure that his staff are at work by, say, 9 a.m. and that they finish by 5 p.m. He should discourage his second-in-command from permitting staff to work late, should be reluctant to incur overtime payments in general and should promote a sense of urgency during working hours. However, upon appointment to a managerial grade, the new manager may find it necessary to adjust his own thinking about working hours as they will obviously be different from those he worked previously.

At this point a brief note about time spent on dictating letters and other work could helpfully be made. Some managers still draft letters to customers and reports on applications for advances, etc. in long hand. This is a ridiculous waste of time and there is no excuse for not training oneself to dictate everything. When writing lending reports (see Chapter 4 'Documentation and advising') it is best to marshall one's thoughts and get the typist to produce a rough copy in double spacing. However, the manager's eventual aim must be to dictate fair copy from the outset – there is far too much pressure on his time without adding to it unnecessarily.

The manager's working day is controlled by that day's particular events. Often it may conform to the above-mentioned periods but it has to be accepted that longer hours may be required, perhaps over a prolonged period. There is a balance to be struck between the time spent in the office and the time spent outside it with individual customers. Customers will hope to find the manager in his office when they need him to resolve an immediate problem over the phone. The requirements of the bank demand his presence in the branch at certain times. Nevertheless, it is highly important that adequate contact is maintained with business customers and the manager should make a positive effort to visit their premises once a year. (This important area is discussed in more detail in Chapter 6.)

Business lunches

Time away from the branch includes time spent on business lunches and the like – functions which are often one of the more enjoyable parts of the job. However, whilst they can be a pleasant change from branch routine, such affairs normally involve at least an hour or two of work and should be approached on that basis. It is a good idea to conduct the business discussion associated with the lunch in the manager or customer's office prior to going to the restaurant so that the business can be transacted away from social distractions. However, this is not always possible and managers should be aware of various points which may arise if business has to be conducted in a restaurant.

Good preparation is important because papers customarily available at an interview will not be easy to use in a public place. (For example, it is probably unacceptable to spread the customer's balance sheet over the table!) Having arrived well briefed, the best procedure is to get the business discussion over as soon as possible so that both parties have time to relax afterwards and time can be allowed for second thoughts to surface. After the first few minutes of pleasantries, the manager should therefore introduce the business aspect by asking if there is anything the customer particularly wants to discuss or by raising the subject if he already knows what it is. The majority of customers will appreciate such an approach because this is, after all, the main purpose of the lunch. An alternative can be to discuss generalities until the coffee arrives before broaching the subject of the business, but this has disadvantages. Firstly, time is running out for both parties – there are other things to attend to and the restaurant may be near to closing. Secondly, if drinks have been consumed before the meal and wine drunk with it, operating efficiency can be below par. Such a time is obviously not the best moment to make decisions. There will always be people who will take advantage of a social occasion and it is best to be fully capable of coping with these sorts of customers at all times. On the other hand, if a manager wishes to obtain agreement from his customer about a difficult matter he may feel that it is at this stage in the proceedings that he can elicit a satisfactory response!

However, on the whole it is good practice not to make final decisions over lunch unless there is absolutely no doubt about the matter. There is no reason why a decision has to be taken then and there. Whilst it is sensible to give an indication of how one is thinking, it is entirely reasonable for a manager to say that he needs a little time to consider what has been discussed and that he will get in touch again with his customer shortly.

SECRECY

Bankers are bound by law to keep the affairs of their customers confidential, and customers rightly expect that nothing will be divulged about their accounts. The observance of this requirement is so integral to banking that it may not be something which is at the front of a manager's mind upon being appointed to a branch. It is, however, highly important to bank business. In essence, it is a simple doctrine – if a banker discloses nothing about any customer's affairs then he can be liable to no one. In practice, it is somewhat different because, from time to time, he will be asked, or for his own protection will wish, to divulge information about accounts. The law has recognised this by admitting that the duty to maintain the secrecy of customers' affairs is not absolute and that there are situations in which customers' affairs can be disclosed (Tournier *v.* National Provincial and Union Bank of England 1924). These may be summarised as being:

1. where disclosure is under compulsion of law;
2. where there is a duty to the public to disclose;
3. where the interests of the bank require disclosure; and
4. where disclosure is made by the express or implied consent of the customer.

Any disclosure will normally arise under the fourth heading. Disclosure under any of the first three headings will be a matter of consultation between a branch and its head office. The bank will be well advised to obtain the written consent of any customer who requires the bank to disclose details of his affairs to a third party.

Status enquiries

Replies to status enquiries are a common exception to this rule as customers are considered to have given their implied consent to such action by the fact of opening their account. However such replies can, of course, only be given to other bankers or to one of the few officially recognised trade enquiry agents, e.g. Dun and Bradstreet. Any enquiries received from parties other than bankers should be referred back with a request that they be resubmitted through the party's bankers.

Telephone enquiries – third party

Real difficulties can arise with telephone enquiries. Ordinary third party enquiries can be treated in the same way as postal requests, i.e. resubmission through a bank can be requested. A problem might arise, however, if for example, a jeweller were to phone to say he has a cheque drawn by a branch customer and wants to know if it will be paid so that the customer, who is in his shop at the time, can take the goods away. The customer may come to the telephone to instruct the branch to tell the jeweller that he is good for the amount of the cheque but unless positive identification can be made the branch should say nothing. Even with satisfactory identification, the branch will need to be wary. The most that can be disclosed is to say that if the cheque were in order and in the bank's hands at that moment, it would be paid, adding that should the customer die or any other legal bar arise before the cheque is presented then the bank will be unable to pay it. The jeweller must make his own decision in the light of the bank's best reply. The special presentation of the cheque may be his safest action.

Telephone enquiries by customers

Care needs to be taken when customers telephone enquiring about the balance of their accounts or about other personal matters as such enquiries may be fraudulent. Whilst the bank is obviously anxious to assist its customer unless positive identification can be established then it will have to refuse to disclose the information requested. An explanation of the bank's position must be given, coupled with an offer to write the same day advising the balance, etc. to the customer's known address.

Telephone enquiries – bank branches

Enquiries from other bank branches telephoning to establish whether a cheque will be paid or not give rise to the same difficulties of identification. The routine to follow is to check the telephone number of the enquiring bank by reference to a directory and return the call. Given that funds are available to meet the cheque, then the bank is able to make a cautious reply (as with the jeweller) to the effect that the cheque would be paid if they had it in their hands at that moment and if it were in order.

The enquiring bank will understand that this is as far as the response can go because if other cheques are presented before the cheque in question there may be insufficient funds available when the cheque in question has to be met and it may then be dishonoured. Banks are not permitted to reserve funds to meet an unpresented cheque. There may be other bars to payment, e.g. the cheque may be stopped by the drawer. Some banks do not permit telephone enquiries of this kind to be answered.

Disclosure

Errors over disclosure can be time-consuming and costly. The second-in-command needs to thoroughly instruct staff on the topic of secrecy and test their memories on it periodically. New entrants to the bank sign a document undertaking not to disclose the bank's affairs. This formal undertaking ought to be accompanied by an explanation of the areas in which they may be at risk – as the pitfalls which can arise when answering enquiries may not be apparent to them.

In general, it is unlikely that a deliberate disclosure will occur. More often it is in casual conversation that things slip out which should have been kept quiet. When subjects are discussed where a banker knows that his bank has an interest which may be unknown to the other party he must keep silent. From the marketing aspect, the maintenance of secrecy is vital since any local feeling that a branch is not to be trusted in this respect will obviously have an adverse effect on business.

SUMMARY

Even if a bank official has been involved in branch banking for many years prior to his managerial appointment he must not think that he can walk into his new job without doing any preparatory work for his new role. However, in some areas he will not be able to prepare himself as the new job will be quite different from anything he has previously experienced. Advance knowledge of the various subjects mentioned in this chapter can make all the difference between a good start and an unsatisfactory one – and the latter may be difficult to correct later on. When looking at the management of bank branches one can often see situations where problems could have been avoided if the manager had established himself correctly in the first place. Those first years of managerial responsibility are crucial to a successful career as a branch manager.

CHAPTER 3

Bank relationships

'If a home be divided against itself, it cannot stand'
Mark 3:25, *The Bible*, AV

The relationship between banker and customer is discussed in many text books but it is rather more difficult to find books tackling the relationship between a bank manager and his head office. The establishment of a sound rapport between head office officials and their branch managers is obviously important if a bank is to be an efficient business and to achieve optimum profits.

A good relationship helps to produce a well-motivated, efficient manager but it is wrong to assume that a good relationship will develop naturally. This kind of rapport needs careful cultivation. Mutual respect is a vital ingredient in this relationship, as is the need to co-operate rather than taking an 'us and them' attitude towards each other. The wider the gap between the two parties the poorer the overall performance of the manager will be. The head office of the modern bank contains a vast store of knowledge which the bank manager cannot possibly carry in his head. If a manager seeking some of this specialist knowledge is treated as a nuisance or in a deprecating manner he will be disinclined to ask again for similar information. On the other hand, he obviously deserves a rebuke if he frequently enquires about matters that should be within his competence. Providing each party understands the parameters within which their opposite number is working mutual respect can be established.

THE MANAGERIAL APPOINTMENT INTERVIEW

The bank manager's relationship with head office commences before he arrives at his branch. The foundations are laid at the new manager's interviews with his general and regional manager. (These take place prior to the manager's arrival at the branch and it is at the interview with the general manager that the appointment is actually confirmed. Often the selection of the candidate has been made prior to interviewing him.) New managerial appointees may not previously have had the opportunity to discuss matters privately with either a regional manager or a general manager. These first interviews can help to develop the manager's feeling that he has a team of professional bankers over him whom he can respect. This will be a different interview from those the candidate has encountered previously when being moved from one minor post to a slightly higher one in another branch. From the bank's point of view, it is a golden opportunity to explain what is required of a manager and to motivate him at a time when he is most receptive.

Well within living memory the appointment of a manager to a branch was a very big occasion in some banks. The appointee might have been received initially by an assistant general manager and then passed on to a general manager who would have made the formal appointment. He, in turn, would have introduced the appointee to the chief general manager who would have spoken about the overall considerations in a manager's work. Following this, the appointee would have been introduced to the chairman of the bank to receive his congratulations. Then the new manager would be passed back down the line again, each time being asked whether there was anything else he wanted to know about the branch or his new position. The new manager could then have been taken to visit the personnel department and also to meet his lending controller. Emerging in the street some three hours after the time of his appointment he could have felt rather bemused but he would certainly have known that he had arrived so far as the bank was concerned – and that he knew what was expected of him.

As bank business has expanded the use of this gentlemanly method of appointing staff to management has declined. The task is now streamlined and delegated. Banks will vary in how they approach the matter today, but one can usually assume that initially the appointee will be interviewed by both his future general manager and his future regional manager – who may or may not be in the same building or city. This will be followed by discussion with the lending controller and the personnel manager. What has not changed in all this is the kind of person coming forward for management; they will still have the same aspirations as their predecessors and the same need for firm initial direction to capitalise on their motivation. The person who must be responsible for providing this initial direction is the general manager.

THE INTERVIEW WITH THE GENERAL MANAGER

The general manager's reputation will go before him and the new appointee may have been warned of any bad traits he has such as bad timekeeping or frequent failure to brief himself properly about new candidates. This kind of behaviour will obviously adversely affect a relationship between the general and the branch manager right from the start. However, given a correct degree of professionalism in the conduct of the interview then the general manager will start the appointee off on the right track and ensure that his keenness to do a good job is undiminished.

The general manager might begin the interview by saying something along these lines: 'Everyone has been impressed with your performance in the bank, Mr Black, and I am of the opinion that you are now sufficiently experienced to take on a managerial responsibility. As you know, we are considering you for the management of our Millchester branch. Are you happy to move to that branch, and do you feel competent to undertake managerial responsibilities?' Having received an affirmative reply, he might continue: 'Good. Now, this branch, although small, is a busy little place and its eleven staff are kept fully occupied. The town cannot be regarded as a developing area but I nevertheless consider it a good place for you to gain managerial experience.' A broad description of the type of business at the branch might follow, together with an outline of any major problems within it and of the general level of deposits and lending, thus giving Mr Black some deeper insight into what he is about to take on. The general manager might well go on to say 'I want you to realise that this is not just a routine interview, nor is the work you are about to carry out of a routine nature. You are about to undertake the responsibility for the branch, and that responsibility starts from the moment you walk down the banking hall on your first morning. Our customers, be they private or business, will be entirely dependent on your judgement and response to their problems. Consequently, your actions may well affect the livelihood and well-being of a significant number of people in the town. Your prime aim will be to run a profitable business and the manner in which you achieve that will reflect upon the name of the branch and bank. I expect to hear that you are running the branch in a welcoming manner in accordance with the bank's policy. You are not going to get anywhere nowadays unless the service you provide is friendly and technically sound. However, the bank does not expect any new manager to produce dramatic improvements in a short space of time. That is not in the nature of banking. What I want you to do in the coming months is to settle into your new responsibility, get the feel of it, organise your day to meet the needs of the business and, by the way, to be on your guard against anyone who thinks they can try to put one over on the bank now it has appointed a new man. Incidentally, when I said 'settle' I did not mean 'retire.' Once you have come to terms with the business, the regional manager and I are going to be looking for results. Do not forget, either, that there is a big support system available to you and that your lending controller will always be willing to point you in the right direction if necessary. I am now pleased to appoint you as manager of the branch at a salary of £*x* with effect from today's date. I wish you every success during your time there.'

Obviously the impressions new managers take away from this interview will depend upon how carefully the general manager describes their new duties to them and on the warmth of support expressed for them. Not every general manager conducts this first interview well, with the result that numerous branch managers assume office lacking the necessary briefing on how to make a real success of the job. If new managers do not understand the ground rules of good management, or do not feel the bank has confidence in them, they can get off to a poor start – which could stunt their development as good managers.

MEETING THE REGIONAL MANAGER

The meeting with the regional manager will probably be fairly similar, though it will examine the nature of the banking at the branch in question in more detail. If the regional manager comes across as distant from the branch manager their future relationship will be adversely affected. (The days when employees regarded officials above them with awe are now gone: respect will only be accorded to senior staff if they demonstrate a professional and helpful approach to those working beneath them.)

THE LENDING CONTROLLER

Moving down the line of management the manager will come next to his lending controller – usually a very able person, probably responsible for the lending and sundry other affairs of twenty-five to thirty branches. He will be the manager's immediate superior and it is essential that they establish a good working relationship. The lending controller will have mentally divided his wards into three divisions. In the first division are those managers he can rely on to run their branches well and to report accurately; the second division will contain those who normally perform well but give moments of anxiety; and the third division will contain the names of a few people whom he has to watch carefully in everything they do. A manager's objective should be to stay in the first division, if only because it makes for a much happier life all round.

Obviously, lending within a branch bank must be conducted in a satisfactory manner and this can happen right from the start if managers follow a fairly simple rule: in the first year of management the only advances agreed must be those which fall within normal lending criteria (see Chapters 4 and 5): everything else should be declined. Such a policy does not work to the disadvantage of customers. The manager is not expected to become involved in marginal lending propositions and he must not create sticky or bad debts. If by the end of the year the manager has a 'clean' lending book the controller will be well-satisfied. Furthermore, having declined a sufficient number of borrowing propositions the manager will have educated himself about how to act in such situations and will not need to hesitate about turning down uncreditworthy proposals in the future.

During the first twelve months he should establish a habit of meticulousness when making reports to the lending controller or when making applications seeking arrangement to borrowing facilities. (One obvious reward of high standards is that the manager won't have to go home at night worrying about some error which should never have occurred in the first place.) If such reports are to be received sympathetically by the lending controller they should be succinct, should establish the main points of a situation and should not gloss over unfavourable aspects of a proposition (see also 'Documentation and advising' in Chapter 4).

The lending controller has an important role to play in the new manager's development. Whilst he cannot be expected to act as a nursemaid, he ought initially to be prepared to guide a new manager on matters which in a year or two he would rightly expect the manager to handle himself. A manager knows that the lending controller can always be reached by phone should the need arise. Difficulties can occur if the new manager is reluctant to consult his superior for fear of displaying ignorance over something he thinks he should be able to tackle on his own. Such a reaction, whilst understandable, is one which will do neither the manager, lending controller nor the bank any good. It is important that the manager recognises the danger of such a situation as his managerial career may be subsequently dogged by his having got off to a poor start which early supervision could easily have put right. A bank's best interest will be served by the lending controller meeting with the new manager, preferably in the latter's office, on a quarterly basis during the first year of the new appointment. This ought to be a purely general discussion about what has been agreed and declined, and it should be regarded as a routine training process for an employee in a new environment. The cost to the bank will be amply repaid in the years ahead.

A lending controller will inform the manager at their first meeting about the general condition of the branch, its good and bad points and will single out matters which he thinks require attention and about which the manager ought to have advance knowledge.

THE REGIONAL STAFF MANAGER

The staff manager of the region will probably be keen to meet his new manager as it will give him an opportunity to welcome him to the area and to discuss the overall staffing position in the region, with particular application to the branch in question. The current situation at the branch ought to be covered in sufficient detail to ensure that the new manager knows the sort of thing he will be facing. The staff manager may be able to supply helpful information about the career, capability and general personality of the second-in-command. His comments about the adequacy of the staff will also be of use to the new appointee, particularly in relation to the usual duties of securities, international work, cashiering and more junior duties. The branch manager should be informed of any imminent transfers of staff and should be put fully in the picture about when new staff will be sent to make up the full complement. The manager may also learn from the staff manager of any adverse environmental factors likely to affect morale at the branch, for example, overcrowded premises, poor public transport, etc. Some people believe that a manager should not be forewarned of impending difficulties or given the personal opinions of another party, which may or may not be accurate. However, it is usually helpful if the manager learns as much as possible about the branch 'warts and all' before taking it on.

Managers should be aware of the kind of information the staff manager can provide so that they can bring up any points which the latter fails to mention; some staff managers are more forthcoming than others. As both individuals will probably have to share the solving of many staffing problems over the years it will help if they start from a good foundation of mutual respect and trust.

THE CHIEF INSPECTOR'S DEPARTMENT

Having seen the afore-mentioned officials, the new manager will have now met all the people to whom he will mainly be responsible whilst in office. The many other departments of a clearing bank are mainly service departments, e.g. training, legal, and organisation and methods, and these provide expertise to be drawn upon when necessary. However, the chief inspector's department, which is responsible for the security of the bank and the enforcement of the bank's operational regulations, should certainly be kept at the front of one's mind. It is a prime managerial duty to ensure that the department's rules are obeyed within the branch. Indeed, serious neglect of these rules will lead to loss of managerial office.

There are a large number of regulations which the second-in-command is expected to supervise on a daily basis. As already stated, the vital regulations are those concerned with cash, keys and strong-room. If these are followed precisely then it is difficult for the more serious offences against the bank to be committed by staff or public. The observance of regulations will not, of course, by themselves prevent a raid on the branch but by keeping to the key regulations, for example, the outer doors and staff doors from the banking hall will be controlled and will create maximum difficulty for any thieves. In the same way, proper key control by all staff engaged in handling cash will not only prevent fraud or accidental loss but will act as a protection to staff engaged on this work.

Managers should remember that adherence to the procedure laid down by the chief inspector's department will not only minimise the risk of fraud or defalcation but will also protect each member of the staff from criticism from superiors. The procedure for cash and keys should claim the manager's closest attention. However, more often than not the manager comes into office already fully aware of the regulations regarding the branch so all he has to do is to ensure that they are enforced.

Inspections

From time to time a head office inspector will visit the branch and carry out a routine check to ensure that the bank's regulations are being met. The inspection is in the form of an audit, at the end of which a report will be presented to the manager pointing out any areas where there is room for improvement. Inspection reports may be expected to cover all aspects of the branch, such as the state of the premises, the state of the lending and the accuracy with which the bank regulations have been followed. It is then up to the manager and his second-in-command to ensure that the improvements which the report requires are made. In the event of the inspector finding serious defects in the running of the branch he may well return to the branch after a short period to ensure that these particular matters have been corrected. A good inspection report can confirm to the manager that he is running his branch on the right lines. Such a report will also be welcome at head office level as evidence of the manager's competence.

SUMMARY

Having considered the relationship between, and the separate roles of, the manager and his head office, it must be reiterated that it is above all the way in which the branch is managed which will ultimately determine the well-being of the relationship.

The first three chapters of this book have been concerned with the need for a manager to understand his role upon taking over his branch and the need for him to observe procedures which will ensure good organisation of the branch. In Part Two the manager's relationships with his customers will be examined in more detail.

PART TWO

The borrowing customer

CHAPTER 4

The borrowing customer – general considerations

'Words pay no debts'
Troilus and Cressida (Act 3, Sc. 4), Shakespeare

The prime requirement of any branch manager is that he should be a good lender, able to identify worthwhile borrowing customers, to make a satisfactory assessment of their needs, and to ensure that in deciding whether to advance funds or not he is following the policy of his bank and is achieving a sound position. The satisfactory outcome of an advance lies in it being repaid within its original time-scale without resort to any security that may have been given by the customer, and without the need to place any pressure upon him to complete his part of the contract. At the same time, the advance should have been made at a rate which will yield a fair profit to the bank.

The new branch manager will normally have had experience in lending money prior to his appointment but his role takes on a significantly different nature as soon as he becomes responsible for the entire lending of his branch. He will have to account to his head office for the disposition of hundreds of thousands of pounds across his customer base and to able to explain the many daily individual lending decisions he has made. There is no way in which this work can be conducted satisfactorily unless the manager has a very clear idea of the way in which a borrowing proposition should be assessed, together with a formula for approaching all requests for bank money. Once the right procedure has been mastered, then the decision-making function can be relatively easy in the majority of cases. (Such a formula is described later in this chapter under 'The lending assessment'.) If a manager fails to establish in his mind the correct procedures he may well find himself with many sticky accounts which are going to cause difficulties with repayment and which will involve him in wasting valuable time. There are always enough uncreditworthy people around to give a manager sleepless nights if he is foolish enough to lend the bank's money to them.

The types of uncreditworthy customers can be divided into two categories. The first comprises those customers who genuinely believe that they can finance a particular object which they wish to achieve but in fact cannot – for example, those who have not done their sums accurately or even at all. The second is made up of those customers who know very well that they have little or no chance of achieving the necessary repayments – for example, those who are desperately short of money and who present a persuasive but false proposition in the hope that it will induce the manager to lend. A self-employed customer, for instance, might offer repayment from the proceeds of work in hand which he knows he will receive in cash and not pay into his accounts. It makes little difference in the long run to the banker which section he lends to – in either case he will finish up with a bad debt. The problem should never be allowed to arise in the first place. Managers should always be on guard against seemingly plausible stories from customers whatever their background. People desperate for money or determined to get it by fraudulent means will not walk into the manager's room unprepared. (See 'The con man' in Chapter 5.)

The lending banker must ensure that the facts his customer has given him are thoroughly authentic and reliable. For instance, if repayment depends upon a lump sum from a certain source then the manager must make enquiries of that source as to the correctness of the sum, must check that there are no other claims upon the money and must ensure that it will be sent direct to his branch for the credit of the customer (thus avoiding any danger of misappropriation). There is nothing more important when assessing a lending proposition than ensuring one makes a critical and worldly-wise judgement about the customer's likely repayment of the loan. Managers are under no compulsion to advance money unless entirely satisfied with the proposal and they must be able to say 'no' as soon as they have the responsibility of lending the bank's money. A branch manager who is not capable of doing so will not retain his job for very long.

THE CUSTOMER'S EXPECTATIONS

Before describing the method of assessing banking propositions, it is worth considering what the borrowing customer is expecting of the bank manager when discussing a proposition. The customer is not only looking for a supply of money but he or she is also seeking assistance generally as to the best method in which to repay, the manner in which to take the funds (e.g. on loan or on overdraft) and advice on the proposition as a whole. Such advice needs to be factual and objective in its content. Bankers frequently deal with unfortunate situations where honest customers, whether personal or business accounts, are faced with a shortage of funds, possibly through no fault of their own and in circumstances which are distressing. In these situations it is vital for the branch manager to keep his feet firmly on the ground, as he may be the only one of the people involved who can still remain objective. He has a duty to his bank to ensure that when lending their money his mind is not swayed by emotional considerations.

However, the borrowing customer does have a right to expect that his bank manager will understand his financial problems and will look at those problems from his point of view as well as from that of the bank. The customer should receive the benefit of a sound appraisal of his position. Such appraisals cannot be made unless the banker is prepared to spend time in gaining a reasonably comprehensive knowledge of what his customer proposes. Customers do not always present their facts in the most straightforward way and it is important that the manager draws out through questioning the facts behind the proposition. This will ensure that both the bank and its customer are entering into liabilities which can satisfactorily be met.

It is often easier for a manager to understand the financial problems of a customer with a private account than one with a business account since dealing with the latter usually requires deeper analysis. It is necessary to discover how a customer regards his own business and the problems associated with it. The manager also needs to understand what makes an office or factory tick in order to decide the extent of the help he can give. Business customers who receive such understanding are likely to be more appreciative and to yield higher profits for the bank in the long term. It is more detrimental to the bank than is always immediately apparent if managers fail to display a close enough interest in the business customer's affairs. Manager's competence is often discussed outside the bank by those with whom they come into contact and a poor reputation can be hard to shake off.

DECISIONS ON BORROWING PROPOSITIONS

Judgements on borrowing propositions are rather a subjective matter: the manager may agree to lend to one customer but not to another although both may have submitted the same proposal. Customers will come to him under all sorts of pressures, disclosed and undisclosed. They may be big companies or individuals of small means. Our new man at Barretts Bank, Millchester must feel confident, when agreeing to lend, that the proposal will work out satisfactorily – and that confidence must be built on concrete facts such as a set of audited accounts and not on specious hopes. It doesn't matter how many noughts are on the end of the figures requested: the manager must be able to give a satisfactory answer to the question 'why did you see fit to make this money available?' He should be able to reply that he did so because there is a source of repayment available and that he has a security in case repayments are not made. If the manager is in any doubt he can ask his second-in-command for an opinion. Writing the proposal down in report form can also help clarify the viability of the proposal. Any proposal must stand the test of good common sense. The question needs to be asked 'can I rely on this course of events happening?' If the answer is 'no' the manager must not agree to the proposition.

Banks are often criticised for lending money to customers when right from the start it is unlikely that they will ever be able to repay the loan. No manager will be happy if he makes an advance to a company for an unsound venture and then has to appoint a receiver for it and see 100 people lose their jobs – especially if the company would still have been in business but for the bank's support. Managers can, of course, lose money through no fault of theirs or their customers – as happened on many occasions in the West Midlands during the depression in the early 1980s. Nevertheless, in normal circumstances managers are not paid to take risks with the bank's money.

THE LENDING ASSESSMENT

The manager at Millchester branch, about to conduct an interview in which he knows a borrowing proposal will be put forward, might well write across the top of his note-pad the four words 'man', 'amount', 'repayment', 'security'. He might also add the fifth word 'cost'. ('MARS-Cost' see p.44). These words can be used to identify the many requirements of a lending proposition and should become so well established in the lending banker's mind that he will soon not need to write them down: they should spring to his mind automatically. Use of this formula will help to ensure that the manager has covered all aspects of the proposition, irrespective of the order in which the customer has outlined them to him.

'Man'

Trustworthiness

The word 'Man' is meant to convey what is possibly the most important aspect of the proposition – whether 'man' actually stands for man, woman, child, limited company or partnership, etc. This aspect is the capability of the borrower to carry out his proposal and it is fundamental to the whole issue of lending money. With the private account customer this may simply mean that he should be honest and trustworthy, and have established these characteristics with the bank over a period of not less than six months. Honesty is obviously an essential quality when it comes to dealing with financial matters and it is important that the banker discards any proposition where he is not entirely satisfied that the customer is trustworthy.

If there have been any factors in the past conduct of an account which have caused a banker to doubt the integrity of his customer then this should trigger an alarm in the manager's mind during a lending interview. It is unwise to believe that a person previously found to be untrustworthy will change his character when coming afresh to the bank for an advance. All too often bankers have acted sympathetically in a situation where previous experience has indicated that the customer is uncreditworthy. Once a customer has proved to be uncreditworthy it is pointless to enter into another lending proposition – unless there are most unusual circumstances surrounding the proposal, for example a major increase in the customer's assets or income. However, even such changes as these would be insufficient grounds in themselves for the manager to loan further money. People's characters do not necessarily change when their income does, and there are many examples of football pools and bingo winners who go through their winnings at great speed. Managers should always be extra cautious after a bad experience with a customer.

Capability

Having dealt with honesty we must consider 'capability' as a requirement of the borrowing customer. This means capability on the part of the customer to execute what they intend to do. The manager must decide whether customers have sufficient technical expertise to carry through the business in which they are engaged, whether they are prepared to put in sufficient time to ensure the success of the business and whether their determination to conduct the business is likely to be affected by any factors such as drink, sex or gambling. (It is not, of course, possible for the manager to ask his customers the last question outright but it should not be overlooked!) If the conduct of the account shows a sudden inexplicable change for the worse then it may have been caused by one or more of these factors.

On one occasion a bank manager lent funds to a customer to buy a hairdressing business. The account ran in a satisfactory manner for a year or two and reductions were regularly made to a loan account. Then, the nature of the account suddenly changed in that the amount paid in each week was considerably reduced. It diminished to such an extent that the repayment of the loan fell into arrears. The customer was quite unable to explain why her takings had declined and the manager agreed to a moratorium on the loan repayments for a few months in the hope that the business would revive. Subsequently, the manager discovered that the business was in fact doing as well as it ever had done but the customer had an impecunious boyfriend who was accepting gifts and money from her at the bank's expense. In the end the shop had to be sold to repay the bank, (whereupon the boyfriend quickly disappeared from the scene). There was no way in which the bank manager could have foreseen that this sequence of events would occur. However, it would be extremely unwise for a bank manager to lend further money to this sort of customer.

Attitudes towards borrowing customers

It is useful to remember at this stage that customers asking for money from the bank often still regard the bank and its manager with some awe. They may have little idea what the bank requires to know about their proposition, the likelihood of it receiving a receptive ear, or the probable outcome of the situation. The bank manager needs to develop the skill of guiding the conversation so that he obtains the information he requires, whilst at the same time allowing the customer to explain matters in his own words. It is important that the customer presents his case in his own way, even though it may take somewhat longer than the bank manager would consider necessary.

It is a good idea to clear up any mystery where it exists, by explaining to borrowing customers the areas in which the bank needs to have information, i.e. the amount that the customer requires to borrow, how it is going to be repaid and whether any form of security will be provided in support of the advance. Once the customer is aware of these considerations he will understand that, given a satisfactory proposal along these lines, there is no reason at all why the bank will not be willing to assist – particularly as the main part of the business is to put funds out to customers at a profit. An informative discussion along these lines can be very helpful to the conduct of bank business and the satisfactory repayment of an advance. (Obviously, with sophisticated customers who have borrowed money in the past, and perhaps run substantial businesses, there will be no need for such an explanation.)

The amount required and its purpose

The second word that the manager wrote on his pad was 'Amount': it is important for the bank to establish exactly how much the customer requires and to be quite certain that this is the correct amount that ought to be lent in the circumstances. It is obvious that if a business man asks for too little money to finance a venture he will shortly be forced to return to the bank with a request for further funds. Where such situations occur they are often evidence of a bank manager's inability to assess the proposition properly in the first place. Similarly, when a private customer borrows funds for the extension of his property, for example, it is important to ensure that the amount he is requesting is adequate.

Whilst there are some customers who ask for an amount which is insufficient to cover the matter in hand there are also plenty of others who will ask for too much, believing that the bank will always on principle decide to give less than the amount requested. This is a complete misconception – the manager's main concern is to determine what is the right amount that should be lent in order to provide adequate finance. However, it is bad practice to provide funds in excess of what is required if adequate margins have been allowed for contingencies.

If customers are working to a sensible budget but one which does not inhibit their activities then this is likely to yield better results all round than if they are lent an excess of funds. Granting more money than necessary to customers can lead to slack financial control, particularly in the early stages of a venture, and this can often end in money being wasted. It could even lead to a request for further funds which would have been unnecessary if proper control had been exercised by both parties in the first place.

During the course of establishing the amount required the manager must also ascertain the purpose to which the money is to be put. There can be no question of the bank remaining ignorant of how its funds are used. In the event of a customer refusing to disclose the purpose, discussions should be terminated and the advance refused. (The purpose of an advance is considered in more detail in the next two chapters: 'The personal borrower' and 'The business account borrower'.)

Repayment

The third word on the pad is 'Repayment' and in this area the manager needs to ensure that both he and the customer are completely satisfied that the repayment scheme for any advance can be satisfactorily implemented and eventually concluded. It is imperative that the source of repayment of any advance is established before the funds leave the possession of the bank and pass into the hands of the customer. Once this has occurred, the bank is very much in the hands of the customer. Even if the customer is considered trustworthy and capable it is still essential that the bank knows where the repayment is coming from, its timing and how long the advances will be outstanding.

Should the customer suggest that the terms for repaying the advance be deferred to a later date this must normally be resisted. The time to negotiate all the terms of an advance is before the money is lent: discussions afterwards will always place the bank in a weaker negotiating position.

Security

'Security' is the last word on the pad and this must be taken in one form or another in the majority of advances. (For more information on securities see Chapter 7). A distinction needs to be drawn here between banking and pawnbroking. In pawnbroking, the broker makes an advance to the depositor of an asset expecting it to be repaid with interest within a specified term. If at the end of that period repayment has not been made he is quite happy to take the asset into his possession and sell it. Banking does not follow the pawnbroker's procedure in any way. Security simply complements a known, sound source of repayment and it will only be realised should the source of repayment fail for some unexpected reason. The pawnbroker does not worry about the source of repayment; the banker knows that it is at the heart of his assessment.

When considering a proposition where a repayment scheme is doubtful although security is available, the banker would normally decline the advance, suggesting to his customer that the security be sold in order to provide the funds. This would prevent a situation where the banker lends the money, finds his doubts on the repayment scheme well-founded and then has to persuade his customer to sell the security to repay the bank. Such a situation is likely to create a poor relationship between banker and customer. Had the proposal been turned down in the first place the customer would have avoided interest charges and the relationship could have remained good.

Banks seldom have to fall back on securities and this may in part be due to sound assessments. It will also be because the customer is anxious not to lose the security. The existence of the security requirement ensures that the borrower maintains a healthy interest in the repayment of the advance. When considering unsecured advances the banker must realise that if he were to agree to one not only would he be without an ultimate source of repayment but that he would have placed the bank entirely in the hands of the customer in this matter. If the customer in these circumstances turns difficult and does not repay the advance for any reason then the bank's only recourse is to costly, and possibly unsuccessful, litigation. It is therefore vital when agreeing to an unsecured advance to ensure that all aspects surrounding the advance are completely satisfactory and that the customer has sufficient assets to fall back on should the repayment scheme fail.

Nearly all personal borrowing (apart from formalised loan schemes) should be covered by tangible security. The same applies to business borrowing until the banker is able to see balance sheets strong enough to support the level of borrowing required. It is unlikely that balance sheets in small companies will have the strength to support unsecured borrowing or to support borrowing which is secured only by a debenture over a company's assets.

Interest and charges

The other possible word on the writing pad is 'Cost' and this covers interest and charges relating to any agreed advance. These should be agreed at the same time as the facilities are negotiated. Customers will expect the bank to mention the cost of the advance at that time and failure to do so may bring difficulties at a later date. If, for example, they consider the rate of interest or commission to be unfair the bank may have to yield ground and accept lower rates than it would have done had the matter been agreed at the proper time. Furthermore, a feeling of resentment may remain.

'MARS-Cost'

The five words that our manager wrote on his pad before his interview form a mnemonic, 'MARS-Cost'. If the manager carries this in his mind as lending interviews progress and mentally ticks off each aspect as it is covered then he will probably have obtained all the information that is required. He will then avoid the embarassment of having to telephone his customer later on and ask for additional information which could have been obtained at the initial interview.

After the manager has agreed an advance he should write to the customer setting out the terms of the loan and mentioning any action that the bank requires the customer to take prior to making the advance available. Customers can easily overlook some of the critical points raised in the discussion and a letter can serve as a useful reminder. Bankers sometimes forget that the time their borrowing customers have available for dealing with financial matters is fairly limited due to the pressure of other activities – and this is particularly true of small companies. It is therefore helpful and business-like for customers to receive written confirmation of the agreement into which they have just entered.

LIMITS – DISCRETIONARY AND OTHERWISE

Now that the manager has a formula for approaching a borrowing interview, the question remains as to how far he can commit his bank. Although there is no maximum limit on the amount the bank will lend, the manager will need to apply to his lending controller for permission on any advances which are above those covered by his personal discretionary limit. A discretionary limit is the maximum amount the head office of a bank has agreed that a manager may lend to individual accounts without reference to themselves. Individual discretionary limits will be determined by the size of the branch concerned and the experience of the manager. They are considered confidential and it is unwise for a manager to disclose the size of his discretionary limit outside his bank.

Unfortunately there are managers who do allow their discretionary limit to become public knowledge and this can have unfortunate results. For example, the manager's limit can be compared with another local manager who has been equally indiscreet and a comparison could be drawn, even though this would be an inadequate basis for decisions about the competence of the bankers in question.

More significantly, customers knowing the extent of a discretionary limit will often put a proposition to a manager designed to fall just within the known limit. They believe that it will be much easier to persuade the manager to agree to such a proposal if he does not have to refer the matter to his head office. This is an unfortunate development. There can only be one bank view of a lending proposal and generally a manager's opinion should correspond with that of his head office were the circumstances known to them. Occasionally there are marginal cases where a manager can lend successfully in circumstances which would not receive formal head office approval.

Establishing of limits and speed of agreement

It is essential to fix the 'limit' which the bank has agreed to advance to any borrowing customer, whether the amount falls within the manager's discretion or otherwise. The amount must be recorded in all the relevant parts of the bank's bookkeeping and particularly on any computer print-out showing the state of the account. Limits also need to be established for any engagement into which a bank enters on behalf of a customer, e.g. where it guarantees its customer's action in some way or other and thereby enters into a liability on the customer's behalf. Limits may therefore relate to overdrafts, loans and engagements, and will set the maximum exposure that the bank has in respect of a particular customer. (A bank has the right to dishonour any cheque drawn in excess of a negotiated limit. It will not always exercise this right and the method by which a decision on this is reached is dealt with more fully later on in this chapter under 'Dishonour'.)

Where the situation at the time of an interview is straightforward, the manager can agree the advance and set the limit then and there. The customer can then leave the bank knowing that the funds they require are available to them, subject to the completion of any security arrangements. If the manager wants time to consider the proposal, or the total required is outside his discretion and therefore needs the approval of his head office, he will need to tell his customer that he will require a few days to consider the matter, and that he will get in touch with him again shortly. There is no need to bring the head office aspect into the conversation.

There will be plenty of occasions in lending interviews where the manager will be sure that the obtaining of head office approval is no more than a formality. In such cases, there is no reason why the manager should not give the customer a general indication of the likelihood of approval so that the customer can have reasonable confidence about the bank's acceptance of their request. The quicker the bank can respond affirmatively to the customer's request the more efficient and professional it will appear in that customer's eyes. However if the manager does not like the proposition, or requires further information before he is convinced of its creditworthiness, the request should either be declined immediately or the customer informed about those areas which are in doubt.

It would be wrong for the manager not to give the customer any kind of idea of how he views the proposition during the course of a lending interview, but this need not stop him taking time to consider the matter further before giving a definite answer. The impression he does not want to give is that he is acting as a post office between the customer and his head office. The manger's job is to make his own personal assessment of the situation and then, if necessary, to sell the idea on behalf of his customer to his lending controller.

DOCUMENTATION AND ADVISING

The preparation of branch documentation necessary to obtain head office approval for a borrowing proposition should be treated as a matter of priority. The customer will be awaiting the bank's decision in order that he can proceed with the proposals. The report should be clear and concise if it is to persuade a lending controller to agree the proposition. If the manger adopts the practice of writing his report in the same order as the 'MARS-Cost' formula, he will be able to present the details correctly and in a business-like manner. The report should relate the history of the account, the capability and purpose of the borrower, the amount required and what are the sources of repayment and security. The report will be accompanied by standardised documentation and this can usually be completed without problem.

When drafting his report the manager should remember that a lending controller will be looking at a number of applications for funds every day. The controller will want to be able to agree or turn down a proposition quickly, so the report should clearly convey the salient points which were established during the manager's interview with the customer. He should not need to ask the manager any further questions after reading the report and if he has to do so then it is an indication that the manager has failed to get to the heart of the matter in hand. The manager should be as frank with the lending controller as he expects the customer to be with him. The success of this application system depends on both sides being entirely truthful with each other so that a correct decision can be made based on a balance between the manager's detailed knowledge of his customer and the lending controller's objective assessment of the proposal's viability. A lending controller will soon cease to have confidence in managers he suspects of being less than frank and will be quickly irritated by managers who fail to present their cases clearly. The system cannot work effectively once a controller has lost confidence in the manager.

Once the decision of the head office is known to the branch, the manager should immediately communicate the answer to the customer. Once again, there is no need to bring the head office aspect to the attention of a customer – the decision is the bank's as a whole. Furthermore, it should be presented to the customer in that manner whether the manager agrees with the outcome or not. There will, undoubtedly, be times when the manager and his lending controller disagree on a particular proposition and the lending controller's opinion takes precedence. The manager must learn to pass on that disagreeable news as though it were his own opinion – even though he may then receive criticism for the bank's attitude.

DISHONOUR

The bank has the right to dishonour any cheque drawn in excess of a limit or where no lending arrangements have been made in the absence of sufficient funds to meet a cheque. When a decision has been made to dishonour a cheque a certain procedure must be followed to ensure that the balance shown on the account is correct. The dishonouring of a cheque, and especially the first cheque dishonoured is a grave matter, as it will affect the creditworthiness of the customer in the eyes of the payee. This is obviously a particularly important consideration in the case of business accounts. Equally, a dishonoured cheque drawn for a small amount may have a more damaging effect in the eyes of the payee than one drawn for a large sum. A thorough search of bank work is therefore necessary to ensure that the account has not only been posted correctly prior to the dishonour of a cheque but that all relevant information is available before the decision to dishonour is taken.

The manager needs to have a check carried out to see that no funds have been placed in accounts with a similar name, that no funds have been paid in that day which are awaiting credit to the account, and that monies are not due to the account within the next day or so (e.g. a salary credit). The branch needs to be aware of any connected accounts where the existence of credit monies could affect the decision. Similarly, managers need to establish whether there are any items held in security or safe custody which need to be taken into consideration.

The general standing of the customer and the length of time he has conducted the account satisfactorily are of importance, as are the past interview notes. Such notes might indicate that the customer has funds in a building society or elsewhere which would be sufficient to allow the bank to pay the cheque under advice of the overdrawn position to its customer. A thorough search of bank records along these lines will prevent the bank wrongfully dishonouring a cheque and then having to cope with the consequent problems. It is also important to clear the bank's letter-box first thing in the morning and also at closing time. It is not uncommon for customers to place credits into the box during the course of opening hours and these should be posted to the account on the same day.

The manager must check any temptation on the part of the staff to carry out a less than thorough search of bank records prior to returning a cheque, perhaps due to pressure of business. Managers cannot assume that this work is invariably carried out properly.

Although the bank is not obliged to telephone a customer prior to returning the cheque (and it would be unwise ever to give any indication that a bank was prepared to do so) there may be times when it will be in the bank's interest for such a call to be made. Customers can easily forget to pay in money which is available or make an error in their calculations and this can quickly be put right. A brief telephone call can be the most business-like approach in the circumstances and can prevent subsequent criticism that the bank should have been more trusting.

Control of uncreditworthy accounts

When a cheque has been dishonoured through the lack of funds, a letter should be sent to the customer advising him of this fact and requesting that in future he refrains from drawing cheques in excess of the available funds. If a second cheque is dishonoured then a further advice should be sent stating that if a cheque is drawn again which has to be dishonoured for the same reason then the bank will take a serious view of such conduct and may ask for the account to be closed. If a third occasion occurs then the bank must certainly come to a decision as to whether to continue conducting business with this customer or not. A customer whose cheques are regularly dishonoured through lack of funds is of no use to a bank and might well cause a bad debt if the bank inadvertently pays a cheque for which no repayment can be obtained. It is important that the number of such customers is kept to a minimum and a firm line needs to be taken to control this area of work.

Difficulties can arise particularly where the customer already has an unsecured overdraft and the bank is having to dishonour cheques. There is often no easy answer to this situation. The bank may have to put up with it for a while in order to obtain payment, on the basis that it is easier to obtain a customer's co-operation with an active account than with one which is dormant. Nevertheless, where this situation persists then it will be necessary to withdraw the customer's cheque book (perhaps by visiting his place of business or home), and to leave the bank with a dormant debt which it must pursue in the best way it can.

Wrongful dishonour

There will be times when despite taking every precaution a bank finds that it has wrongfully dishonoured a customer's cheque. It is a fundamental principle of the banker/customer relationship that a bank will pay cheques properly drawn on itself by the customer, provided that these are presented for payment in the ordinary course of business and that there are adequate funds available (or agreed borrowing facilities) on the account. If a bank fails in this duty it is open to a claim for breach of contract and/or libel. Such a claim may result in significant damages, particularly in a case where the account of a trader is concerned and the cheque is in favour of a supplier who, on the strength of receiving notice of dishonour, withdraws credit terms which have been arranged. The fact that cheques have been returned previously will not mitigate a claim against the bank if one is made.

In order to remedy the situation the bank should telephone the drawee bank as soon as the mistake is discovered to advise it of the error. The bank must also speak to the payee, if possible, for the same purpose, and offer profuse apologies. Letters should also be written the same day confirming the conversations. The wrongful dishonouring of cheques does not always give rise to claims and whether it does or not may depend on the promptness and efficiency of the bank once the error is discovered.

Answers on cheques

As stated, claims against banks for damages can be made either on the grounds of breach of contract or libel. The action for breach of contract arises through the actual dishonour of the cheque, whilst the action for libel arises from the answer written upon the cheque when it is returned to the presenting banker.

There is a good deal of case law surrounding the level of damages that may be payable regarding wrongful dishonour on accounts of private individuals and of traders – particularly where the latter can prove an actual loss has been sustained. The branch manager must therefore ensure that the correct answer is always written upon a cheque being dishonoured. Answers of a technical nature such as 'out of date', 'words and figures differ', 'payment stopped by order of drawer' are factual and no harm can come from such answers providing the bank has the written authority of the customer not to pay a stopped cheque or it can see that the cheque is irregular. Before marking a cheque 'drawer deceased' the bank should have seen a death certificate or be quite certain that its source of information is reliable.

The straightforward answer which can be written on cheques dishonoured for lack of funds is normally 'refer to drawer' or 'refer to drawer, please re-present'. The latter answer shows that there is a better chance of payment upon representation of the cheque because the bank has reason to believe its customer will have put the account in sufficient funds by that time. If there is no reasonable hope of funds arriving then 'refer to drawer' should be used.

It is not uncommon to see cheques going backwards and forwards between the drawee and the presenting bank a number of times marked 'refer to drawer – please re-present'. Unless the drawee has good grounds for expecting funds, this ought not to occur and the drawee bank should on the second presentation delete the words 'please re-present', adding the date, thus returning the cheque with the answer 'refer to drawee'. This will leave the payee of the cheque in no doubt about the situation and it will be up to him to pursue his money direct with the drawer. The words 'please re-present' need to be used with care for they may induce a payee to extend further credit to a customer in the belief that the cheque will be met on representation. If the answer 'refer to drawee' had been given then the payee might have acted differently.

In cases where one party to a joint account is suffering some kind of financial disability, the answer on a returned cheque needs particular care. For example, where a Mr Alan in a joint account Alan and Chapman is made bankrupt the answer for the account should be 'refer to drawer, Alan in bankruptcy'. The words 'refer to drawer' are now almost universally recognised as indicating that the drawer has insufficient funds to meet his particular cheque. Therefore, where the words have to be used in a connection other than insufficiency of funds they need to be followed by an explanation of the situation, for example 'refer to drawer, winding-up petition presented'.

Uncleared effects

If a customer issues cheques before the bank has had time to clear items on which the cheques rely, then the bank may dishonour the cheques with the answer 'effects not cleared'. The answer will clearly cast doubt upon the customer's creditworthiness in the eyes of the drawee and payee and imply that, were the effects cleared, then the bank would have been able to have made payment. It is unethical for a banker to use this answer in circumstances where he would have marked a cheque 'refer to drawer' had the account still been beyond its limit when the items comprising the relevant credit had been cleared. It is suggested that such cheques be marked 'effects not cleared – refer to drawer'. Payment of cheques drawn against uncleared effects creates a potential liability for the bank if by chance the cheques being collected are dishonoured by the drawee bank and consequently need to be debited to the customer account when they are returned. Therefore, the total of any uncleared effects needs to be deducted from a credit balance (or added to a debit balance) in order to determine the exact position of a customer's account. If the net position is not acceptable then the relevant cheques should be returned.

Money has been regularly lost by banks paying against uncleared effects and whilst the modern computer print-out highlights the uncleared position more effectively than was possible in the past, a manager always needs to be on his guard against giving a customer a sense of false security by permitting payment against uncleared effects to become a habit on a particular account. If such action becomes a regular practice the customer will begin to assume that the bank has an implied agreement to pay such cheques. The manager would then be obliged to negotiate with the customer before ending the practice.

The composition of credits is important in assessing an uncleared position. Where a credit contains, for example, twenty cheques averaging £50 each, all drawn by different drawers, then any risk is widely spread and the customer might be allowed to draw against the majority of the credit. There is a marked difference between that situation and one in which the bank has cheques presented to pay against a credit containing one cheque of £1,000. In this situation the bank will be entirely dependent upon the uncleared cheque being met and would, therefore, be at full risk. The theory surrounding uncleared effects is easy enough to understand but in practice it is a high risk area – as shown by the number of managers who have lost substantial funds by paying against them.

The second-hand car trade is a classic example of a business where single large cheques are paid into a bank account and where the customer needs that money to purchase further cars for trading purposes. In the case of such accounts it would be no surprise to a bank manager to find several cheques presented in the clearing one morning drawn against a single large cheque and to have the customer pressing him to pay them and giving assurances such as 'I've sold another car and am picking up the cash in the morning'; 'it will be all right; the drawer's as safe as houses', 'I've done plenty of deals with him before and his cheques have always been met', 'even if it does go wrong I know where the car is and I can always go round and pick it up again', or 'I've got two other cars going out tomorrow so I can easily put the position right'. When a manager believes tales like this he usually finds the risk he has taken coming home to roost. What is required in such a situation is good, tangible security to fall back on. If this does not exist the bank manager should dishonour the relevant cheques and if there is a further occurrence of the same situation suggest the customer closes his account or transfers it to another bank – which would be equally unlikely to accept such behaviour. It is all too easy to be gullible in these circumstances: very plausible stories are told. An established source of repayment must be identified if payment is to be made against uncleared effects. Even nowadays six figure sums have been lost through lack of care.

Crossfiring

Crossfiring is the practice of drawing against uncleared effects, where the uncleared items are drawn on an account (or accounts) elsewhere of the account holder. It is a most dangerous practice for the banks involved and must be stopped as soon as it is detected. The effect of paying against cheques paid in before sufficient time has elapsed for them to be cleared is tantamount to giving an overdraft facility.

Banks have often been exposed to crossfiring with the intent to defraud and the first thing to establish is whether the customer is innocently misusing the system or is intent upon fraud. If they are innocent then it is probably a one-off situation with the customer obtaining a few days extra credit. However such practices should be stopped whatever the cause.

If there is an intent to defraud then the practice is likely to be of a continuous nature with the amount of uncleared effects gradually increasing as the days go by because it is only by increasing the amount that additional benefit will accrue to the operator of the crossfiring system.

Table 4.1 illustrates a crossfiring exercise in which banks A and B both hold an account conducted by the same customer although the names will probably be different. It will be seen that on Working Day 1, bank A is at no risk, having only received a cheque of £1,000. However, on Working Day 3 that cheque is presented to bank B who pays it against a credit of £1,500 drawn on the A bank account. At the same time the customer cashes a cheque for £400, leaving bank B with a £1,400 risk and an uncleared balance of £1,500. On Working Day 5 a similar set of transactions occurs, leaving bank A with a £900 risk – the £1,000 paid in on Working Day 1 has been cleared. However, in order to obtain benefit, the customer has to increase the amount paid in to £2,000 which, on Working Day 7, results in a risk to bank B of £2,300 because once again the customer has increased the credit by a further £500 to put money in his own pocket. On Working Day 9 the customer attempts the same set of transactions at the higher level which would leave bank A with a risk of £1,800. However, on presentation of the cheque for payment, the manager, having now become aware of what is happening, declines it and returns the cheque for £2,500, marked 'effects not cleared'. However, a £400 cheque was cashed. The effect of the manager's action will be to leave his bank with a cleared credit balance of £700 (£1,100 – £400), whereas bank B, following the return of the cheque for £2,500, will be left with a loss of £2,300.

Both branch managers will need to report the situation immediately to their respective lending controllers and chief inspectors as a fraud has obviously been perpetrated at the banks' expense. The kind of action taken against a customer like that in this example obviously depends on whether or not he can be found. Bank B is going to contact bank A as soon as the returned cheque of £2,500 is received. Bank A can return any cheques presented against the £700 balance marked 'refer to drawer' once it is satisfied that a fraud exists

Table 4.1 An example of a crossfiring exercise

Bank A						Bank B					
Working day	Debit	Credit	Ledger balance	Uncleared effects	Risk	Working day	Debit	Credit	Ledger balance	Uncleared effects	Risk
1		1,000	1,000 Cr	1,000	Nil	1	—	—	—	—	—
3	—	—	—			3	1,000				
							400	1,500	100 Cr	1,500	1,400
5	1,500										
	400	2,000	1,100 cr	2,000	900	5	—	—	—		
7	—	—	—			7	2,000				
							400	2,500	200 Cr	2,500	2,300
9 (a)	2,500	3,000	1,200 Cr	3,000	1,800	9	—	—	—		
	400										
(b)	400	3,000	3,700 Cr	3,000	Nil £700 Cr cleared						
						10	2,500 (Dis-honoured cheque returned)	—	2,300 Dr	—	2,300 (Loss)

(a) Potential.
(b) Actual. Cheque for £2,500 dishonoured.
It is assumed that three working days are regarded as satisfactory to clear cheques.

– there is no chance of the customer suing for wrongful dishonour despite the credit balance! Obviously bank B will return the cheque for £3,000.

The possibility of prosecution through police action still exists, with perhaps some redress to bank B in respect of the credit balance existing on bank A's current account. It would be easy to say that both bank managers had been foolish to allow these transactions to take place but, as already stated, errors can occur, whether due to the heat of a day's business, to pressure exerted by customers or to a clerical error. The example given is a simple illustration of how the risk can quickly escalate between two accounts. It is even more difficult to spot a crossfiring situation where a clever trickster has spent months setting up six or more accounts for the purpose of defrauding banks. He may well be moving funds around every day and may have two or more accomplices signing on the other accounts to disguise the activity. If the above example is multiplied by a factor of ten then one can appreciate the degree of danger which lies in such fast losses. Managers new to office need to be particularly aware of the possibility of this kind of situation arising. Bank managers in the past have lost sums of money running into six figure amounts, although convinced by their customers that their bank was at no risk.

SUMMARY

Having considered the topics in this chapter, it should be clear that essential qualities in successful branch managers are the ability to communicate with the customer and the strength of personality to act firmly. Bankers have to communicate with virtually the whole spectrum of society and must accordingly adjust their manner and approach to each sector. All customers, irrespective of background, need to be able to feel they can relate to their banker and, since it is the bank which wants the business, it is up to the banker to communicate effectively with the customer. Business will certainly be adversely affected if customers do not find themselves received by the manager with understanding and on an equal level.

However, the manager must, at the same time as being approachable, be capable of remaining sufficiently objective in relationships with customers to be able to assess requests for loans in a realistic way. They must always be wide awake to the potential problems which can lead to customers failing to repay loans.

CHAPTER 5

The personal borrower

'The human species, according to the best theory I can form of it, is composed of two distinct races, the men who borrow and the men who lend'
The Two Races of Men, Charles Lamb, 1823

The personal borrowing at a branch is an important part of its business and can be divided into two sections. The first covers all formalised borrowing schemes: for example, personal loans and budget accounts – schemes which have been created by the head office of the bank and to which a set of lending requirements applies. If a customer meets these requirements he or she is automatically lent the money. The assessment of whether the customer meets the requirement is often dealt with on a credit-scoring basis (an explanation of which appears later in this chapter). Formalised schemes are administered as general instalment finance.

Advances which fall outside formalised schemes make up the second section of advances to a personal customer and the reasons for requiring money in this area cover a very wide field. Since the introduction of formalised lending, the manager has been able to delegate that part of his work to his staff, although he must maintain general supervision of it. With the second type of lending, the manager is involved in all individual cases.

THE ASSESSMENT

In the case of formalised schemes the bank has an established assessment procedure but for the other kind the manager will have to make the assessment himself. When conducting a lending interview he should remember that the customer must not be allowed to conceal any facts about matters which could jeopardise the arrangements. He is engaged in a business transaction in which bank money will be lent on terms which should result in a trouble-free repayment satisfactory to both parties. At no time should the manager think that he is doing the customer a favour. It is the customer who is doing the bank a favour by bringing it business. The position is clearly simpler if the customer is already well known to the bank. Unless the customer has been known to the bank for over six months and has maintained an active account then a good rule is to avoid lending money altogether, because it is these situations which can lose the bank a considerable amount of money. In his private life a banker is no more likely to lend money to an acquaintance of short-standing than anyone else is and it is unwise for him to have a different attitude in his business life. Dishonest customers may well attempt to borrow money shortly after an account has been opened and a manager must make certain that he is dealing with a bona fide customer before considering any sort of advance.

If the customer presents his requirements well during an interview he obviously has a better chance of the manager agreeing to his proposition. The manager will be able to see quite quickly that the customer is capable of thinking through his needs and of considering the ways in which they can be met. Nevertheless, there are plenty of creditworthy customers who have not got the skill to make a good presentation and the manager will need to ask sufficient questions to draw out the essential details. There is no reason to suppose that everyone is tutored in money matters or even particularly interested in money. Nor is there necessarily a correlation between intellectual ability and astuteness in monetary affairs. Someone who does not seem particularly intelligent or articulate may display a flair for financial dealings. It is only by face-to-face discussion that a banker can form an opinion in this respect. It is, therefore, important that wherever possible the manager interviews the customer at the bank rather than setting up a lending agreement by correspondence or over the phone.

Purpose

The manager must be satisfied that the purpose of the advance is acceptable to the bank, both from a legal and practical point of view. For example, if trustees request an advance, he will be aware that trustees are not empowered to borrow unless sanctioned by the trust deed and the advance may be declined on those grounds. He may well decide that it would be better for trustees to realise investments rather than borrow money.

There are times when banks do not like advancing funds for stagging a share issue, for example, during periods of credit restriction, and such a purpose would again need to be declined. Another area in which care needs to be taken is when the manager is faced with a request to amalgamate a customer's debts borrowed from other lenders into one account at his branch. This request often arises because the other lenders are pressing for repayment. It is foolish to agree to such an amalgamation as it frees the other lenders from their bad lending and imports trouble into the branch. If a person cannot repay lending taken from one source, then he is unlikely to be able to repay it just because it has been transferred to another. Furthermore, the borrower is usually trying to extend the period of the advance in order to reduce the monthly outgoings, which is a good indication that he is living beyond his means.

Repayment

Some people are by nature careless, helpless, arrogant or spendthrift in money matters. They may make proposals which from another set of customers would be acceptable but the manager must recognise that any advance to these sorts of people will probably be unsatisfactory. Indeed, the bank could actually cause the borrower to get into deeper financial trouble by advancing money which the customer probably will not be able to repay.

In the case of personal borrowers it is usually quite easy to establish the amount needed to fund a proposition or to establish how far it is reasonable to go in the circumstances. For example, if an extension is needed on a house the builders' estimates will testify to the amount required and the manager then only has to determine with the customer how much the latter is able to contribute to the transaction and, if satisfied with that, to ensure that the customer can meet the instalment finance to fund the project. Where repayment is to come from a salary then other outgoings must be taken account of and the manager should not hesitate to ask enough questions to satisfy himself. Care should be taken when the customer is relying on annual bonuses since bonuses earnt in the past may not necessarily continue to be paid at such a high level in the future or may not even be available at all.

Banks are often asked to advance funds in anticipation of monies being paid to customers arising out of insurance claims, legacies and the like. The manager must see documentary evidence establishing that the customer has a genuine right to receive such monies and, if possible, a statement from the solicitor or insurance company indicating the amount which will be received. However, in the early stages of an insurance claim or a winding-up of an estate it may be difficult to determine exactly how much will ultimately be received. The manager needs to proceed warily because customers' expectations are often for a sum higher than the amount they actually receive. It may, therefore, be as well to decide to lend an amount that falls comfortably short of expectations so that in the end neither party is embarrassed.

When considering this type of proposition, the manager will need to remember that, whether it is an insurance company or a solicitor who ultimately provides the funds to repay the advance, these people are not the security for the advance. Where the amounts involved are of a significant size compared with the customer's assets, the bank should have no hesitation in asking for security. The customer's expectations may fail for reasons that could not be established at the outset. If a solicitor's unconditional undertaking for a specific sum can be obtained then it is not necessary to look for security.

Customers: salaried or self-employed

The income of a salaried customer is usually regular and constant in amount. There is every reason to rely on that income being the main source of repayment for an advance providing the employer remains in business and the customer continues to be a good employee. However, with self-employed customers a different situation exists because their income is dependent upon their own business success. Customers with established businesses ought to be able to produce trading accounts showing the income that has been earned over the last two or three years as some indication to a manager of what he may expect to be the customer's future level of income. Such accounts will not show any tax liability and it is therefore necessary to establish with the customer if there is any outstanding income tax to pay. However, there are a large number of self-employed people running small businesses who will either be unable to produce any accounts or who have accounts which may prove valueless to the manager. If, for example, the customer says that the accounts were only drawn up for Inland Revenue purposes and are actually worth more than they show then the manager will not know what to believe. The problems of lending to jobbing builders, for example, are notorious. They, like various other sectors of the self-employed, sometimes do not get paid – perhaps because their work is not up to standard and the customer refuses to pay the full amount. Alternatively, they get paid in cash and have other more pressing debts which get settled in preference to the bank advance.

Overall, the small self-employed, private account borrower is a risk area in which the source of repayment needs to be particularly well established and where an advance may often have to be declined unless tangible security is available.

Undertakings – to provide funds

With short-term, self-liquidating advances the source of repayment can often be satisfactorily verified by making enquiries from the ultimate provider of the repayment funds and having his agreement to send those funds direct to the bank.

Solicitors' undertakings can be relied upon because under the regulations of The Law Society if they fail to comply with an undertaking then they or their firms are liable to make good any loss caused by such failure. However, it is not usual to require security when holding a solicitor's unconditional undertaking; in the case of undertakings given by anyone else, the security aspect needs consideration. Whilst the solicitors can be relied upon to send funds direct to the bank for the credit of a customer's account, undertakings from anyone else do not have the same status and it might well be difficult for a bank to obtain redress against such a third party who failed to comply with an undertaking. For example, it has been known for an insurance company to give an undertaking to send the proceeds of a claim direct to the bank for the credit of a customer's account and then inadvertently, to send the money to the customer when the claim was met. If the customer then fails to pay the money into the bank, the latter's position is difficult – particularly if it has no security. The insurance company would probably resist paying out twice and a difficult situation would then ensue.

Security

Security is essential in all personal borrowing, except in cases of formalised lending schemes or where small amounts of money are involved. As already discussed, security should be taken before money is lent as it may be difficult to obtain later on – and it certainly will be so once an advance has become sticky. However sound a borrower's position may be when the advance is negotiated, unforeseen circumstances do arise which prevent repayment. The possession of a tangible, realisable security will not only avoid ultimate loss to the bank but also provide a useful discipline to persuade the customer to adopt an alternative repayment scheme where necessary.

Despite what has been said in the media, bank borrowing is relatively cheap and its costings do not provide for bad debts in the same way as, say, the charges of a credit card company do. Nowadays there is a trend towards a more relaxed attitude about security from personal borrowers for ordinary loans and overdrafts, probably because there is now so much unsecured, formalised lending. However, the tenet that bankers only lend against security holds true in the context of personal banking. On the whole the manager should only deviate from this policy when there are very convincing reasons for so doing. For example, if the proposition is so strong that it can stand being unsecured. The following example may help to make a distinction as to whether to take security or not.

A customer asks to borrow £5,000 to enable him to purchase a new yacht whilst waiting to dispose of his existing boat. If the bank has lodged with it in safe custody a mixed collection of shares, national savings certificates and premium bonds worth, say, £15,000, then it has evidence that the customer has resources which could meet the debt if necessary. Provided the customer has a good record with the bank it might well agree to make this temporary advance on an unsecured basis, although strictly speaking a charge should be taken over the securities. If on the other hand, there is no evidence that such free liquid assets are available to the customer then it would be most unwise to make an unsecured advance, even though the sale of the first boat was expected to realise a few thousand pounds more than the £5,000 requested to buy the second boat. The proposal sounds plausible on the face of it and could work out. However, if for any reason the bank is not repaid, it has no recourse to the original boat and it may now have been sold. If a full loss is incurred, the bank would have to lend about £38,000 elsewhere for twelve months at normal interest rates in order to recoup the £5,000 loss – and without any profit on the new money. This illustration demonstrates the need for security both as a source of repayment and to maintain the customer's interest in the repayment programme. (Further discussion on aspects of security can be found in Chapter 7.)

THE LOAN VERSUS THE OVERDRAFT

Having decided to make an advance the next decision is whether it should be taken on loan or on overdraft. Where repayments are to come in on a regular basis, monthly or quarterly, there is no doubt that borrowing should be taken on loan, despite possible pressure from the customer for it to be taken on overdraft in order to reduce the interest he will have to pay. If an instalment repayment advance is taken on overdraft then the bank will have to reduce the limit each month and the customer will have to remember what that limit is.

It is quite probable that over a period of (say) twelve months the customer may forget exactly what the limit ought to be for the month concerned and his repayment programme may go awry, possibly leading to cheques being dishonoured. If the advance is taken on loan then it will be reduced regularly by transfers from the current account. The customer will know the amount that will be deducted from the balance each month, and the terms of the advance will be kept. Any advance in respect of property where a customer will be entitled to tax relief on the interest must be taken on loan account, otherwise the relief will not be available.

Overdraft limits for personal account borrowers are more suited to advances which are self-liquidating, which are in anticipation of salary or 'in case of need'. Overdrafts arranged in anticipation of salary should not be allowed to develop into regular borrowing as the customer can get into the habit of living beyond his means. Eventually the borrowing, or part of it, will need to be placed on a loan account with regular repayments in order to get rid of the debt. When the bank calls a halt, the customer not only has to restrict his spending to the amount of his monthly salary but also to find the monthly instalments to repay the debt. The manager should take early action to prevent such a situation arising.

Some customers like to arrange an overdraft limit 'in case of need' should they possibly require funds at some future time and thereby have the assurance that they can issue cheques up to the overdraft limit arranged without reference to the bank. It is, of course, a sensible precaution for customers to have an unused line of credit available if they feel one to be necessary.

PAYING CHEQUES

Before dealing with the actual payment of cheques, it is important for the new manager to be certain that the information on which he is making his judgement is sound and reliable. Much of this will come from computer print-outs and he must ensure that all relevant details concerning his customers' accounts have been input. This information should include all accounts where there is a set-off or connected accounts. As already stressed, it is particularly important to ensure that all information is up to date when considering dishonouring a cheque or writing to a customer concerning an overdraft on his account for the first time. The need for a thorough investigation has already been discussed in Chapter 4 under 'Dishonour' but the importance of such a procedure before dishonouring cheques or writing to customers about advances cannot be overemphasised.

When to stop paying

Nobody in his right senses would hand money over to a virtual stranger in a darkened room and come away with the expectation that he would get it back again. A manager should not part with his bank's money unless he is assured that there is good reason to expect that it will be returned. Generally speaking, customers do not expect a bank to pay their cheques if they are drawn in excess of available funds or in excess of an arranged limit – certainly they have no right to believe that the bank would do so. Any manager will daily be called upon to pay cheques that are drawn outside the arrangements made with the bank. In practice most of these he will be able to meet based on information available to the bank.

The bank is under no legal compulsion to advise a customer of a dishonoured cheque and indeed staff should never commit the bank to doing so. If the customer has not taken the trouble to tell the bank of his position before issuing a cheque for which funds are not available, then he cannot justifiably complain if the bank does not like the situation. Nevertheless, where goodwill needs to be retained and the manager is becoming concerned about potential indebtedness it is advisable to return cheques under advice to the customer. Once again the manager must remember that it is sound policy not to part with money unless there is an established source of repayment. In Chapter 4 this section is dealt with in more detail under 'Dishonour'.

Head office clearing

A large proportion of cheques will be drawn in anticipation of salary and whilst individually the amounts involved may not be great they can accumulate to the point where the situation gets out of hand. Some banks instruct that customers may generally be allowed to anticipate up to a stated percentage of salary and a manager should be guided by this regulation. Opinions vary considerably on what percentage might reasonably be advanced but a figure of between 20% and 25% of the regular monthly salary for established customers is a good yardstick. Such an allowance can never replace a negotiated limit but since so many cheques are presented for payment nowadays without funds available to meet them a practice has developed of inputting internal limits to the computer system to keep the accounts off the daily print-out – thereby keeping it to a controlled length. This system undoubtedly has its drawbacks, but in the pressure of modern branch banking, it is not now possible to write to every customer as would have happened in the past.

A customer with a salary of £800 per month might be thought good for a limit of £200. A limit of £204 would therefore be put in the computer indicating that the salary is received in the fourth week of the month. If the account becomes overdrawn by £200 in the second week of the month this would indicate that the borrowing was already too high and needed investigation, whereas if this happens in the fourth week it would be normal and requires no action by the staff.

Having decided on the percentage of salary which can be anticipated, it is essential to act immediately that level is reached, either by returning cheques or by writing to the customer to ensure that the breach will not occur again. If accounts are not treated in this manner then the branch will finish up with many of its accounts out of financial control. Small, bad-borrowing situations can spring up overnight like mushrooms in a field and unless the manager acts firmly, he can find himself with lending problems which deflect him from pursuing more profitable business for the bank.

Correspondence regarding overdrawn positions

The manner of advising a customer of any unacceptable level of borrowing depends on the seriousness of the position. Often the receipt of a statement showing the overdrawn position will be quite sufficient to ensure the customer corrects the borrowing. Some managers have three standard letters of increasing severity which are sent out as appropriate. Letters regarding unacceptable borrowing should be worded so as not to cause offence. Compare 'Your account is overdrawn £250 and we shall be obliged if you will pay in to correct the position' with 'We think you would wish to be advised that your account appears to be overdrawn £250 and shall be glad if you will explain the position'. The second one would give less offence should the bank have made a mistake.

Instances occur with joint accounts where one customer is creating an overdraft without knowledge of the other. It is prudent to ensure that both parties are aware of the position. With overdrafts on joint accounts held by a husband and wife there is a time-honoured belief that the best solution is to send a letter together with the statement timed to arrive on Saturday morning (over breakfast) in the hope that both parties are there together to consider the matter. Where there is trouble with a joint account of a husband and wife often only one of the two is failing to control the finances. The sooner the other party knows the position the more likely the situation is to be corrected.

CHEQUE CARDS

There is no doubt that the introduction of cheque cards has made the control of personal lending much more difficult. Whilst it is possible to nominate a percentage of salary that the branch will readily allow trustworthy customers to anticipate, this whole practice can be upset by cheques being presented drawn under cheque cards. Payment of these must be made even though borrowing may then rise to unacceptable heights.

Such situations must be curtailed immediately by drawing the customers' attention to the indebtedness by phone or by letter. Although this means increased work it is normally effective in bringing the account back into order, perhaps by the customer agreeing to borrow on loan with regular monthly repayments. Where there is no satisfactory co-operation from the customer then the branch must try to repossess the cheque card – and possibly the cheque book, depending on how bad the situation is. Such customers need to be reminded that cheque cards remain the property of the bank, that the bank wishes to have these cheque cards back and that no further cheques may be issued against them. In very difficult cases, one of the staff may need to call upon the customer to repossess the card and, of course, where fraud is in evidence the police may have to become involved.

Cheque cards have become an essential part of the financial life of the country today and have brought undoubted marketing benefits to banks. Nevertheless, their existence has made it even more important to know whether or not customers are trustworthy. It is unwise to issue a card to a customer who has not kept an active account with the branch for six months or more. In situations where bank policy dictates that cheque cards may be issued to students immediately upon opening their accounts any resultant losses are unlikely to be attributed to the manager by his head office.

LENDING BY CORRESPONDENCE OR BY PHONE

Whilst it is always best to interview a customer before coming to a decision about an advance, occasionally this may be impossible and requests will be received in writing or by telephone. Requests for advances by letter give ample time to consider the proposal and the manager can always write to ask for any further information required. However, some proposals are too complicated to be dealt with adequately by correspondence and in these instances managers should not hesitate to request an interview before proceeding any further. Moreover, if the customer is not known personally to the branch, he may need to be asked to come in for an interview – particularly if the successful completion of the proposal is likely to depend on his ability and trustworthiness. Naturally, the amount involved will also have a bearing on the matter.

There is a great deal of lending business conducted over the telephone. Where the customer and his affairs are known to the manager, it can often be simpler and quicker for both parties to do business in this way. The type of business transacted would normally be where a customer requires short-term accommodation due to an unexpected lack of funds. The danger with telephone calls is that they may lead to decisions based on too little information, particularly if they come at a time when the manager is busy. The manager should feel under no obligation to make a hasty decision and can if necessary say that he will ring back at a more convenient time.

Except in cases of emergency, no telephone calls should be put through to the manager's office during the course of an interview with a customer. The customer deserves the undivided attention of the manager and quite apart from the difficulty of discussing the affairs of one customer in the presence of another, there is a risk of breaking the rules of secrecy.

APPROPRIATION

This book is not the place to deal at length with all the aspects of appropriation of payments. In any case there will be very few branch bankers who are not familiar with the rule in Clayton's Case, which states that, in the case of a current account, the first sum paid in is the first drawn out and that the first item on the debit side of the account is extinguished or reduced by the first item on the credit side. Clayton's Case applies in all situations where a specific appropriation has not been made. However, managers do need to maintain a working knowledge of this rule and there are one or two practical aspects of it which need to be borne in mind. For example, if a customer who keeps two accounts with the bank pays in a credit, he has a right to appropriate the funds to either account as he sees fit. If the customer does not do so then the bank may decide into which account the credit will be placed, though normally it would seek to establish the customer's wishes on the matter.

Another situation which can arise is where a customer who is low in funds pays in a credit stipulating that the funds are to be utilised towards paying a certain cheque. The bank must comply with this instruction, and should it utilise the funds for paying other cheques, thus leading to the dishonour of the specified cheque, then it will be liable to the customer for not following the instructions that had been given.

In general, a customer who pays money into a bank has the right to apply the money as he wishes. There will be the odd occasion when the bank requires a credit to go towards reduction of an overdraft and the customer asks to pay it into another account so that it can be spent. As the customer has the right to appropriate the money, it must then be up to the manager to use his powers of persuasion to achieve the end he requires. He can resort to calling in the whole advance if necessary.

Set-off

Where a customer maintains two (or more) accounts in the same name(s) (in the same 'right'), one being overdrawn and one being in credit, then the bank may at any time look to the net position so as to determine the amount owed to the customer or owed to the bank. When making a decision about paying cheques, it is necessary for the bank to set-off such accounts in this way in order to make a fair assessment of the situation. It is important that all accounts are checked and this includes balances on deposit accounts.

In these circumstances, it is important that the customer understands that the bank will act in this way and that any agreed overdraft limit will be conducted against the net debit figure. Furthermore, the bank has the right to retain the benefit of credit balances if the overdraft limit is reached and the customer issues cheques against them. It is good practice to establish the position in writing with a customer where this situation occurs. In cases where large sums of money are concerned, a letter of hypothecation (set-off) may be taken from the customer in which he formally agrees to the practice.

CREDIT SCORING

With the advent of mass banking in the 1950s and 1960s and the introduction of unsecured personal loan schemes, the pressure on the working day of the average bank manager increased, and it became necessary for him to operate a system under which small personal lending business was delegated to his staff. These credit-scoring systems were introduced by most banks along the lines of those used by credit card companies and finance houses – all of whom offered borrowing facilities to private individuals with whom they often had had no previous connection. (However, banks have an advantage over these institutions in that they have the banking accounts of their customers, and the conduct of a banking account is a valuable guide to the likelihood of repayment.)

Credit scoring has taken many lending decisions away from the branch manager, together with the enjoyable personal consultation that often accompanied it. However, since the role of the manager has been extended in recent years to a wide range of marketing activities – in addition to ever-increasing business – some change has been inevitable. Indeed, experience has shown that on the whole banking customers prefer a credit-scoring system to having to present their application personally across a manager's desk. Credit scoring has come to stay and has also now been applied to the small business sector by some lenders.

The credit-scoring system

The credit-scoring system has been defined as 'the measurement of statistical probability that credit will be repaid'.* In setting up such a system a bank can refer to its experience with good and bad borrowing accounts to assess the various factors in borrowers' backgrounds which have produced such results. A satisfactory credit assessment is shown in Table 5.1 where the information commonly sought on application forms is presented. Against each section of the form a maximum number of points has been placed showing the appropriate value deemed by the bank. There will be a pass mark of (say) 45 for any application and the loan will be granted if the

* Drury, T. 'Lending by Numbers', *Banking World* (March 1984).

customer's details produce that minimum score or over. Each question can be broken down statistically in order to award points – thus the question 'How long with employer?' might be treated as shown in Table 5.2.

Table 5.1 An example of a credit-scoring system

Personal loan application form	Maximum points
Marital status	5
Dependents	10
Age	10
Occupation	20
How long with employer	10
Type of property occupied	15
Years at present address and prior address	5
Date account opened with bank	25
Maximum total	100

Table 5.2 Credit-scoring in relation to length of employment

Under 6 months	1 point
6–12 months	2 points
1–2 years	5 points
2–4 years	8 points
Over 5 years	10 points

The pass mark can be varied in accordance with bad debt experience. However, this should not often be necessary in a well set-up system where the level of bad debts would usually remain below 2% and would often be lower. Personal loan lending rates are of course about 6% higher than ordinary lending rates. This covers the higher bad debt potential.

As already mentioned, personal loans are normally only given to customers who have conducted a satisfactory current account for at least six months. There will be times when a considered decision has to be made because the assessment is on or close to the pass mark. There may be a few creditworthy customers who do not reach the pass mark and who should be given individual attention and there will obviously also be a few uncreditworthy customers who score above the pass mark but whose loans turn into bad debts. However, experience shows that the latter account for a very small proportion of the total and are taken care of in the costing of the system. The whole operation can largely be left in the hands of security clerks who are competent to deal with customers at this level.

Once the personal loan application has passed the credit-scoring test, it is usual to carry out a check with a credit agency in order to ensure that there is no history of writs, judgement debts, etc. outstanding against the intending borrower.

THE CON MAN

A newly appointed manager may be a prime target for a con man although the latter's activities are certainly not confined to inexperienced managers. Whilst some people pass their whole career in banking without coming across a con man there are enough such people about for any manager to need to be on guard against them. People who are intent on fraud may well give the appearance of being trustworthy and competent business persons. They will also be well versed in banking practice, will know the type of questions that a manager is likely to ask about a proposition and will have all the answers ready at their fingertips. Their main goal is to defraud the bank or, occasionally, to conduct an account in order to defraud the public.

Detection of fraud

Using the mnemonic 'MARS-Cost' can be a means of safeguarding against fraud. 'Man' for example: what does the manager know about the person? They may well have just walked in off the street and this will be a danger signal in itself. On the other hand they may unwittingly have been introduced by a respectable customer innocent of their contact's fraudulent purposes. They may even have had an account with the bank for twelve months or more, that account having been set up for the sole purpose of obtaining an advance which they do not intend to repay.

Although an experienced manager can often instinctively sum up people by the time they have walked across his office and sat down he must still establish what is known about the person, the business they conduct or their employment with other people. Proof from reliable sources about the person's credentials is vital before proceeding with any business. Secondly, amount: how much is being asked for (this is likely to be significant) and for what purpose is it required (this will probably appear to be acceptable). These factors need very thorough investigation. The manager can expect cash flows, management accounts, etc. to be produced as a matter of course. If they are said to have been prepared by a chartered accountant then his existence and reliability need to be checked because there may also be professional fraud involved.

Collusion

Turning to 'R' for repayment the same thorough investigation has to take place. Often in a case of fraud a claim will be made that the repayment will come from a fixed source which may include solicitors' undertakings. In this situation the manager should remember that there are several old tricks associated with this practice. For example, the person being interviewed may be in collusion with an unscrupulous solicitor and another party, their purpose being to anticipate the sale proceeds of a property. The interviewee will be vendor of the property and will have exchanged a contract for sale through the solicitor with the other party, the purchaser. The sale price will be substantial. The object is to induce the bank to lend for an acceptable purpose against the solicitor's undertaking to account to the bank for the proceeds of sale upon completion. Once the bank makes the advance, the purchaser promptly disappears, leaving the solicitor unable to comply with the undertaking – ostensibly through no fault of his own as there is no purchaser to complete the transaction. The bank will have a bad debt and since the solicitor will not appear to have done anything irregular there may be no proof that he was party to a fraud.

A similar situation might also arise where the solicitor was in fact respectable, but in this case it would be more difficult for the potential criminal to work the fraud, since solicitors are usually careful for whom they act and they, as well as the bank, would have to be deceived. Potential confidence tricksters will know that it is not normal practice for banks to worry about property inspections when lending against a solicitor's undertaking where sale contracts are exchanged. This being so, they hope to get away with the proposal they are putting to the bank.

Security

It is in the realm of security that a con man's proposal is most likely to break down – if enough warning bells have not already rung in the manager's head. A con man will be unlikely to offer good security, unless he intends to use security which belongs to another person whom he is also attempting to defraud. He will be either seeking an unsecured advance or offering security that is worthless or inadequate. Where the background of a customer or proposed customer is in the slightest bit obscure it is imperative that the manager ensures there is a good legal charge over tangible security. The manager must not permit the bank to be rushed into the advance prior to having secured this charge.

The illustration cited earlier of the solicitor's undertaking that turns out to be worthless describes a case in which the borrower is previously unknown and where the bank finds that the proposal is not based on an adequate undertaking. To avoid such a situation a bank should firstly take a legal mortgage over the property concerned, even though it may be for a very short while. Secondly, the bank should make a physical inspection and valuation of the property. If there is the slightest doubt about the valuation then an independent valuer nominated by the bank should be employed at the customer's expense.

The bank's solicitors should then investigate the title and ensure that there are no impediments to it – for example, undisclosed tenants or others who could claim some right of occupation or contribution to the cost of the property and thus reduce the value or chance of sale. Similarly, the valuation of the property may depend on planning consents which either have not been processed, have not been granted or which are in a different form from that described to the bank. Even having come this far it is not too late for the manager to about turn and refuse the business if attempts to obtain security have revealed the probability of the proposal being fraudulent.

In the writer's experience the con man is usually aged thirty and above. The question that needs to be asked of any new customer of that age group is where he or she has banked previously. If they are genuine, then by that age they must have had prior bank dealings otherwise they would not have enough assets to be able to put forward such a borrowing proposition to the manager. If the interviewee is not able to come up with a satisfactory explanation which can be substantiated by respectable outside parties then the person and the proposals ought to be rejected at an early stage.

It is not unknown for a con man to be introduced in good faith by the manager of another branch of the same bank: fraudulent requests for advances can be presented in a very sophisticated manner. Use of a sound credit assessment investigation should enable a manager to discover where a fraud is about to be perpetrated, often early on in the negotiations. Obviously, any experience of this nature should be reported to the bank's head office with a view to preventing a repetition at other branches. If the manager is in any doubt as to the respectability and trustworthiness of the people with whom he is dealing, he should generally discuss the matter with his lending controller well before any decision is made to advance funds.

SUMMARY

Personal accounts form the bulk of the total accounts in nearly every branch. The marketing of instalment credit schemes has become a high priority in banking today and the related assessment procedure has been simplified by the introduction of credit scoring. As a result the number of borrowers has increased – and so, correspondingly, have the difficulties of controlling advances.

It has become increasingly difficult to prevent personal customers taking unauthorised overdrafts, especially since the increasing use of the cheque card. The maintenance of an effective control system has therefore become even more important. If the number of out-of-order accounts in a branch is above average, it may well be that the control system is imperfect rather than that the branch has an above-average number of uncreditworthy customers. Where there is weak management and/or poor control unnecessary losses will certainly be incurred. The only way to avoid problems arising from personal borrowing is to make sure loans are firmly controlled right from the outset by ensuring there is a sound source of repayment and that security is taken where necessary. It is no good asking questions after an overdraft has been created.

CHAPTER 6

The business account borrower

'Seest thou a man diligent in his business?
He shall be set before kings'
Proverbs 22:29, *The Bible*, AV

Business account borrowers are the most important element in nearly every domestic bank business. They are the greatest users of the bank's deposits and they form the most profitable element in a bank's activity. Business account borrowers will represent a bewildering variety of organisations of all sizes, complexities and capabilities. (It is only necessary to look at the list of companies quoted in the financial pages of a daily newspaper to get some idea of the diversity and the extent of the business world.)

UNDERSTANDING THE BUSINESS CUSTOMER

The branch manager is going to have to deal with whatever segment of the business community happens to conduct its banking at the branch. In some cases, the business activity may be confined to one or two particular industries that are in the locality, but more often there will be a diverse spread of business interests needing attention. The manager is not going to be of use to the bank or its customers until he has some understanding of the workings of those businesses and of the way in which their financial affairs should be conducted. He needs to be capable of appreciating the practical signficance of the facts he is given by a customer and to be able to ask the right questions as a result. Otherwise the manager starts acting as a go-between for the customer and the lending controller, reporting situations without background or analysis and behaving as though his lending controller were psychic!

One way in which a new branch manager should start learning about business accounts is by visiting his well-established, reliable business customers so that he can begin to recognise what constitutes good systems and sound performance. He will then have less difficulty in recognising inefficient concerns and in identifying their problems. No one is going to sit down and teach him how to deal with this area of his work and so he may experience initial problems in making assessments of his business customers' capabilities. Acquiring this skill is all part of becoming a respected and professional banker.

The new manager dealing with business customers will need to develop practical skills in areas where he has previously only had theoretical training. The theory of business management can be acquired from books and from some bank courses but the application of it in practice over a wide range of customers can only really be picked up through practical experience. Unfortunately, in the nature of things, new managers are unlikely to have spent any time outside the banking industry within the course of a banking career and so the new manager usually has to learn as he goes along.

There are substantial benefits to be gained from taking time to meet the customer on his own premises and in getting to know his problems at first hand. Customers who have never been visited by previous managers will probably be only too pleased to show the new manager around. No long-term business can be fully developed between a branch and an important customer without regular visits to the latter's business premises. A reputation for customer care may well result in an enhanced reputation for the branch and in the manager being better able to assess problems or requests for advances as they occur in the future. In the first instance he should visit as many customers as he possibly can, spending an hour or so with them walking round their premises in order to gain an impression of the efficiency of the business and through general discussion to understand how each department works.

CONFIDENCE IN THE ENTREPRENEUR

The first consideration of the manager faced with a business account is to establish how good are the entrepreneurial skills of the people seeking the loan. Much of the banking assessment the manager has to make will hinge on this factor. There is the classic example of the sales and the production managers who, seeing a marketing opportunity, join forces and start up a business which they are quite capable of running whilst the activity is small. However, as the business grows, the two need something more than, on the one hand, the ability to sell and, on the other, the ability to produce. With expansion come more employees, increased stocks, bigger debtor and creditor lists. Consequently, one of the two is going to have to give up his specialisation and turn to the running of the business, leaving either production or sales to an employee. There are cases where both partners are reluctant to do this as they have not appreciated in the first place that such a development would occur. Unless one of them is capable of acquiring the necessary management skills the business will falter – as many branch managers have discovered in the past. Inadequate management can also occur when a well-run business is affected by the death of its principal and the duties are taken over by a member of the family. Although the person who takes over can sometimes turn out to be more able than the deceased, there are plenty of occasions where they are incompetent and the bank manager finds that what was once a good business is now faltering. If these two sorts of situations exist they ought to be quickly identified by the branch manager in the course of general discussion.

At the risk of over-simplification it is fair to say that most businesses go through the same trade cycle. They turn stocks or services into debtors, and require the latter to pay at the right time in order for the business to pay its creditors, to buy more stocks or to pay for more services to keep the cycle going. This all has to be done at a profit sufficient to enable the business to gradually expand – for without expansion any business will have difficulty in maintaining its momentum. The complexities of managing the trade cycle obviously increase with the level of business and the manager needs to be satisfied on two counts. Firstly, that the product or service is one which will continue to be in demand, and secondly, that the trade cycle at its current level is competently managed. The sales figures for the previous year show how demand is progressing and the manager must form his own opinion as to the likelihood of the sales figure being maintained in the future. Assuming that the manager is reasonably confident about those running the business and about any market influences that bear upon it, he will need to ask the following further questions about the trade cycle in order to form an opinion of its viability. For example, in respect of the stock, has the company had any difficulty in obtaining supplies and is it dangerously dependent upon one supplier? What is the likely level of the price of supplies in the forthcoming twelve months and what effect would a price rise have, i.e. can the gross profit margin be maintained? Is there an effective control of the level of stock – unless there is, cash flow may be tight and may disadvantage other aspects of the business.

Regarding manufactured stocks, the bank needs to know that production runs to schedule and that delivery facilities to the customers are adequate. It is always worthwhile knowing the failure rate in any production programme as repair or re-manufacture of products can be a significant cost.

THE BUSINESS ACCOUNT AND DEBTORS

How well a business controls its debtor list is of prime importance to a bank when it is conducting that business account. The manager will need to establish how the company pursues its debtors. Are customers invoiced regularly and on time? How long are they given to pay and what action is taken on aged debts? The manager should do his best to insist that the system operates with maximum efficiency because obviously only then will it benefit bank and customer alike. The degree of sophistication necessary to control a debtor list varies with the size of the business and the size of the business will determine whether the bookkeeping function should be computerised. Once computerised a business should be producing an age analysis of debtors and creditors each month and this should be available for inspection by the manager so he can quickly determine whether or not debtors and creditors are well controlled.

CONTROL OF CREDITORS LIST

Turning to the creditor lists, a manager needs to be certain that all creditors are paid to date. This does not only apply to trade creditors but also to creditors of the company for overheads such as rates, VAT, national insurance, PAYE, etc. When asking for an up-to-date amount due to creditors the manager should be specific about what he wants otherwise the customer may produce a figure which only includes trade creditors. In situations where money is tight many businesses tend not to pay creditors such as PAYE and National Health Insurance so that a substantial liability can arise in these areas. The bank needs to know about this particularly when any lending becomes doubtful.

BUDGETS

Having ascertained the situation in the area of debtors and creditors a manager will be forming a fair opinion of the customer's competence in managing their business. To be quite satisfied that the customer is planning his business along the proper lines and can project the results of the current or next year's trading the manager should ask to see the revenue and capital budgets for the year. These budgets will show that the customer has considered what is going to be spent on capital items and has ensured that the cash flow of the business is sufficient to meet those projects. If a customer is unable to produce such budgets he will probably encounter difficulties at some future date. The manager's insistence on seeing such forecasts may force the customer to consult the company's accountant which could in itself be a good thing.

ASSESSMENT OF BUSINESS LENDING PROPOSITIONS

Obviously, the easiest forms of lending propostions come from customers whom the manager already knows and who are probably already borrowing. The manager will be familiar with the background of the business and its history and will have visited its premises so that the request for new or additional finance probably conforms with the wide picture of general business expansion. The manager has a more difficult task when approached by a business customer who has not borrowed before and if the business is completely unknown to him he needs to be especially careful. If it is already an established business, it may be transferring from another bank and the question of paramount importance is why the proprietor expects to be able to borrow the money from a new bank when he has presumably been unable to get his present bank's agreement to it. Many requests coming from former customers of other banks will be an attempt to bolster up an already difficult financial position. The manager of the new bank will need to have very good reasons for taking a different view. He should recognise trouble when he hears remarks such as 'you have the reputation of being the best manager in the district'!

Establishing the background

This stage of the assessment is equivalent to that dealt with under the word 'man' in the mnemonic 'MARS-Cost' (see page 39), and is best examined by describing a situation in which a new manager is considering a proposition from a new business account.

Prior to the first interview the new customer may have made a presentation in writing setting out the details of the company's background, and this obviously helps the manager form some advance idea about the business. If no such information has been provided the bank must establish the origins of the business and how it has developed up to the present time. The manager must get to know the company's products or services, how they are sold and to whom, the strength of the market and what the potential borrower considers to be possible areas for expansion of his business. It could also be of interest for the manager to know who the main customers and suppliers are as this can help him assess the degree of dependence placed on any one particular customer or supplier. Again it is useful to know if any new products or services are in the pipeline and to discover whether the business can rely on a steady market for its products.

Above all, as mentioned earlier, it is vital that the bank is aware of the level of management capability within the business. The age, qualifications, training and experience of the principal personnel need to be established since if the bank does agree to the lending proposition, the performance of these personnel will be critical to the repayment of the advance.

Purpose

The purposes to which bank money can be put has been extended considerably in the last two decades. It was not so long ago that any borrowing for a period of longer than five years was considered to be a long-term lending proposition and was rarely contemplated. Today, the commercial banks are prepared to lend money for up to twenty years but on the whole they maintain their traditional role in providing short-term capital for commerce and industry.

During the course of the discussions on the background management structure and products of the business, the purpose for seeking the bank's assistance will become apparent. The manager should be satisfied that the customer's aim is sound and is achievable within the overall capacity of the business. Great care needs to be exercised when the purpose is to embark on a completely new activity within an existing business or for the finance of a completely separate start-up (see 'Start-up finance' on p. 98). Also although the purpose of the advance is unlikely to be illegal it must be ensured that it falls into line with bank policy.

Applications for advances for capital expenditure to be taken on overdraft should normally be resisted and the customer should be required to take such advances on loan. Requests from a profitable, healthy company to finance additional working capital are quite straightforward banking business, whereas, obviously, requests for the same purpose from a company short of working capital and in a poor trading position are not usually acceptable. The bank will not wish to advance money when a company has a troubled outlook as frequently such situations can take a long time to resolve and can waste a lot of the manager's time.

Premises

The manager also needs to be certain that the premises from which the business is conducted are adequate. He needs to know about their size and condition, whether they are rented or freehold and their location and value. It is also important that existing premises are adequate for future as well as current trading. The last thing the bank will want having agreed a loan is for the customer to come back to the bank fairly shortly afterwards asking for further funds to finance a move into enlarged premises. If the premises actually constitute the security on which the advance is to be made then this whole area is of even more importance.

Employees

The number of employees currently employed by the business must be established. In addition, the manager needs to know whether the business is anticipating any increase in staff in the near future so that he can assess what impact there may be from this quarter on general finance. Where specialised skills are required by a business, it is important to discover whether or not the necessary labour is available in the locality in which the business is situated. Even in times of high unemployment there are always areas where it is difficult to obtain labour – both skilled and clerical.

It is unwise to assume that customers have thoroughly thought through the issues of employment, premises and kindred problems in relation to the project for which they are seeking finance. A really efficient businessman will have done so but many otherwise quite creditworthy customers do not always go into matters as thoroughly as they should.

The amount required – gearing

Gearing is the ratio between the amount of money that the proprietor has in the business and the amount of money that is being borrowed.

With a partnership, the amount of money in the business will be shown on the partners' capital accounts. With a company, the amount of money will be represented by the total net assets at the bottom of the balance sheet. (Balance sheets are dealt with in greater depth on pages 84–89.) One of the objects of the manager's assessment is to ensure that the customer does not become too heavily geared, and the bank will usually regard a maximum of one to one as being enough.

Once a business starts borrowing more money than is already invested in it the borrowing will become increasingly difficult to finance. For example, in a bad case where a bank has considerably more money in the business than the proprietor has, the capital repayments and interest may be amongst the largest expenses in the accounts. The structure is therefore out of balance, resulting in there being insufficient funds to finance other aspects of the business. At the same time, the proprietors can become disillusioned with their employment because nearly all their efforts are going into repaying the bank and not into their own pockets or towards making proper provision to finance trading. Such a situation can lead to disaster.

Many chartered accountants will say that too often banks permit a level of borrowing far in excess of the proprietor's stake and that the banks should ensure that such stakes are adequate to avoid the consequences of over-gearing. This may be true but it can be explained by the bank's desire to retain accounts which would otherwise transfer to a competitor willing to assist despite poor gearing. Insistent customers can be difficult to handle. It is sometimes argued that by giving a charge to a bank over his home a customer has increased his stake in his business and the bank should match his commitment. However, this does not always follow as although the customer has increased his risk the money borrowed is still subject to interest charges and will have to be repaid, whereas a cash injection by the proprietor does not.

To illustrate the position that can arise with gearing let us take the accounts of a private limited company with net assets of £100,000 and see the difference that arises if it wishes to borrow £150,000 over five years or £80,000 over the same period. (See Table 6.1)

The figures in Table 6.1 demonstrate that having added back the depreciation shown in the profit and loss account, the company has £80,000 after tax available to finance its business in respect of capital expenditure. The figures assume a straightforward capital and interest repayment scheme so that in the first year £51,000 is required to finance £150,000 of borrowing whereas £27,200 is required to finance £80,000. On the face of it, either of those figures looks within the company's capability. However, the heavier borrowing takes 63.75% of the total amount available whereas 34% is taken within the smaller borrowing.

Table 6.1 The accounts of a private limited company

Sales last year		£1,000,000	
Net profit (after tax)		£70,000	
Depreciation		£10,000	
Gross cash flow		£80,000	
Funding of advances at 14% over five years			
	£150,000		£80,000
Capital reductions p.a.	£30,000		£16,000
Interest first year (gross)	£21,000		£11,200
	£51,000		£27,200
Percentage of cash flow	63.75%		34%

The question the branch bank manager would now have to ask is 'Can the company manage to conduct its business in the forthcoming years with only £29,000 left over after the bank has had the £51,000 required to fund the advance?' The answer to that question is likely to be negative because the company is almost certainly going to have other capital items to cover in the forthcoming year(s), e.g. increases in stock, capital reductions on hire purchase and any increases caused by an expansion in the business or by suppliers whose costs cannot be passed on. The repayment figure of £27,000 obviously looks healthier on the borrowing of £80,000 and bears a much more sensible proportion to the total net asset figure of £100,000.

However, just because the gearing looks right the residual figure of £52,800 which would be available to the company is not necessarily sufficient to fund its non-revenue expenditure. (The latter should include a provision for contingencies which are bound to arise during the course of any trading year.) The adequacy of the residual amount can only be assessed by having a clear understanding of the demands likely to be made upon it. It is a feature of an assessment such as this that the bank is unlikely to see the profit and loss account much before six months after the accounting date. Therefore, the directors need to be able to tell the bank what has occurred in respect of capital expenditure during the intervening period. They should also be able to give a good pointer to the coming months prior to the end of the current trading year and well into the next trading period.

Profit and loss accounts

All businesses will have a profit and loss account each year and managers must look at a series of these in order to establish how the business has been progressing. Profit and loss accounts are of little use to a bank until they have been audited by a qualified accountant. The manager should try to obtain the accounts within six months of the accounting date so that he possesses early information as to the progress of the business. (Insistence on this will also benefit the proprietors since they too need confirmation by audit that the position they anticipated being in at the end of their trading year has been achieved.)

Managers look at profit and loss accounts to ensure that the gross profit is adequate to cover the overheads whilst at the same time leaving sufficient net profit to finance capital expenditure and to cover the trading position in the forthcoming year(s). The accounts should show an expansion in sales at least sufficient to keep up with inflation. The gross profit margin ought to be maintained, although where there is a significant increase in sales the percentage rate may ease due to larger individual sales having to be negotiated at a lower price. Gross profit margins are subject to fluctuations arising from both internal and external factors, e.g. the rise (and fall) of suppliers' prices which can or cannot be handed on to the customer, the need to expand or maintain the client base in the face of competition leading to lower prices, the fact that the basic costings may be wrong, the nature of changes in the pattern of discounts allowed and received, transport cost variations, etc. Many businesses find difficulty in maintaining their budgeted profit margin due to unexpected interplay of market forces and to inefficiency on the part of personnel. The manager should seek an explanation of any significant changes and enquire about the expected gross profit margin and sales level in the next period. For example, a drop in the gross profit rates from 25% to 22% on £1 million sales reduces the profit by £30,000. Sometimes insufficient attention is paid to this aspect.

Overheads

The overheads of the business should be seen to be consistent with its general level of business and, if they are, there should be no difficulties in this area. A word of warning is needed about situations where the level of directors'/partners' salaries appear to the manager unduly high. This is an emotive area and a manager should be very cautious about raising the matter – banks have lost business through insensitive handling of the subject. On the whole proprietors of private businesses have every right to draw as much as they can, for that is the purpose of the business. The manager should only question the situation when excessive drawings upset the financial stability of the business.

Whether the net profit is adequate or not may be determined by adding back the depreciation as this is a bookkeeping entry and not an expenditure item. Aids to assessing the adequacy of a net profit figure are dealt with under the section 'Budgets, management accounts and cash flows' later in this chapter. All that need be done here is to reiterate the observation that just because the cost of funding a project appears to be comfortably within the aggregate of net profit plus depreciation, it is not necessarily sufficient to warrant an agreement for a lending proposal. The bank must be in possession of a capital expenditure forecast in order to have satisfactory knowledge about the trading position.

BALANCE SHEETS

This is not the place to go into the detailed composition of balance sheets – any new recruit to the position of branch manager would be expected to be quite familiar with them. (Indeed, he should be able to read them as easily as a musician can read a sheet of music.) However, it must be stressed in this context that the balance sheet is a prime document upon which a lending assessment is made. The manager must read them thoroughly and ask questions about any item on them with which he is dissatisfied.

Fixed assets

The size of fixed assets will depend on the nature of the business and the valuation of those assets will be a matter of establishing facts. With freehold properties they may remain in the accounts at cost and there is a hidden reserve when taking their likely realisable value on a sale. Conversely, plant and machinery will appear at their cost less depreciation, the net figure bearing no relation to the price that could be obtained in a forced sale. Experience in recessions has shown that the value of plant and machinery depends upon their type and degree of specialisation: it may be impossible to sell them for anything other than their scrap value. Cars and commercial vehicles are the other main section of fixed assets and it is useful to know the company's policy on replacement. Providing the business keeps the mileage on vehicles down to a reasonable level and limits the period of ownership then a value of 25% of the balance sheet figure will not be far wrong.

Current assets

Turning to current assets, stock needs to be seen to be adequate to operate the business successfully. However, it can be difficult to control (perhaps because there is insufficient personnel or time to devote to the matter). The manager needs to ensure that he understands the stock position and that the funds necessary for cover are available. Where stock levels are significant, stock-taking should have occurred in the presence of the auditor. The latter should then be able to confirm that the balance sheet figure represents the cost of saleable stock and that unsaleable stock has not been included. Work in progress is often included in stock and it is important to ensure that this has not been overvalued.

Where a manager has any doubt about figures in the balance sheet or on the profit and loss account then he should obtain his customer's permission to speak directly to the auditors. They will normally be most helpful in providing any additional information that is required.

The total of debtors in the current assets is always an important part of a balance sheet assessment. The ratio of debtors to sales gives an indication of the average time they are taking to pay but it is better to request an age list of debtors. This can often be provided from computer print-outs and will give a much fuller picture of the position. If the business does not have such a specific debtor control system then the manager can suggest that one is introduced. Auditors are usually willing to set one up. A debtor age list ought to show very little money owing over the business's normal credit term period. It will also give an indication if there is a serious bad debt problem.

Current assets can often include figures in respect of money owing by, or invested in, subsidiary or associated companies, and a cautious approach is necessary in these circumstances. It is wiser to assume that the entry is worthless until the manager can prove otherwise.

Such proof can only be obtained by looking at the audited accounts of the businesses concerned and making an assessment of whether or not they are able to meet their liability to the customer under review. It is not uncommon to find that such entries contain funds lost in other ventures which have not been written off. Such a situation can arise out of desire to maintain the appearance of the balance sheet. Occasionally, when delving into the underlying features of the balance sheet entry, it will become evident that the structure of the balance sheet has been considerably upset and that a business which appeared to have a good working capital is in fact in difficulties.

Some companies make short-term cash investments whose value can easily be assessed. Such investments, coupled with the balances of bank accounts in credit, etc., generally comprise the total of the current assets of the business out of which the current liabilities have to be met.

Current liabilities

The main item of current liabilities will usually be the creditors. Trade creditors should bear a proper relationship to the level of purchases. By taking the ratio between purchases and the total of trade creditors one can prove whether or not the business is paying its accounts regularly. An age list of creditors should be seen wherever possible and a similar assessment can be made as with debtors. It is always useful to ask if there are any pressing creditors and, if so, for what reason. In cases where the working capital position is poor, it is particularly useful to ensure that there are no writs in existence. The figure for creditors may contain every creditor of the company or the creditors may be divided into 'trade', 'other creditors' and 'taxation and social security'. Under the latter heading will be included PAYE, National Insurance and VAT amounts outstanding at the date of the balance sheet and the manager should be satisfied that these payments in particular are up to date. (As mentioned earlier it is very common for parties which are short of cash to lapse in payment on these items because of the pressure to pay trade creditors in order to remain in business.) As this section of creditors will be treated preferentially in the event of a winding-up, it is important that the bank sees that they are kept under control. (Where the accounts show a sound position overall it is probable that these creditors have also been kept up to date.) Corporation tax should normally be shown separately and will probably be payable in the following January. Hire purchase and bank loans will represent the amount payable by the business in the current year and any entry for a bank overdraft speaks for itself.

There are, occasionally, entries in respect of amounts due to associated companies or group companies and enquiries should be made regarding the surrounding circumstances. Both asset and liability entries of this nature may contain amounts relating to current trading between the parties involved or may concern other matters already discussed under 'Current assets'.

Working capital

The difference between the total of the current assets and the total of the current liabilities represents the net current assets/liabilities or 'working capital' of the business. Although there can be no hard and fast rule about this relationship, a ratio of two to one would normally represent a very good position. More often the ratio is less than that and businesses frequently operate on what seems to be a very low level of working capital. Managers should tread with care when faced with balance sheets for such businesses as they present the bank with considerable risks. The manager will either have to refuse to lend or endeavour to extricate the bank from its current lending situation as best he can. Proprietors or directors of such companies will be spending a lot of time trying to collect money from their debtors – even prematurely in some cases – in order to keep the business going. This will mean that less time is being spent on developing the business.

In other words, in such circumstances the whole business operation becomes overstretched. The conduct of the bank account is likely to have deteriorated, with cheques possibly being returned or credits being received at the last minute to cover cheques already presented. These are clear warnings that all is not well with the business and the manager must investigate the position straight-away. In such situations businesses can go to the wall overnight and the bank needs to anticipate this by acting promptly in order to protect itself from the worst.

Creditors – falling due after more than one year

The remaining liability sections on the balance sheet will contain creditors of amounts which become due after more than one year (this may only be seen on company balance sheets). Entries in this section will contain all long-term liabilities including bank or outside financing. The amounts shown will be the total amount less the amount due for repayment in the current year – the latter appearing under current liabilities. There may be an entry in respect of amounts due to a parent company. The manager should establish the terms on which that money has been received and whether there are any repayment or interest terms which could affect the bank's assessment of the balance sheet. Directors' loans to a company can also appear and similar enquiries need to be made about these.

Balance sheet – capital and reserves of companies

A bank manager will normally be able to take the capital and reserves stated as being true representations of the actual situations. Just occasionally there may be some calls outstanding on ordinary share capital, in which case their current position should be enquired after. The accumulated sum on profit and loss account (revenue reserve) represents the total of past profits (or past losses) made in the business from inception. Sometimes the total of share capital is low in relation to the total of net assets and the amount standing to profit and loss account is, conversely, substantial.

It can be argued that in order to present a well-balanced picture of the business, a transfer should be made from profit and loss account to share capital by the creation of further shares. Improving this aspect may give creditors cause to regard the company in a better light, since the creation of additional capital protects funds utilised in that respect from being distributed. In an ordinary, well-run, private limited company such action may be nothing more than a cosmetic improvement but in a public company relying on its Stock Exchange listing and outside shareholders, the matter will be of greater importance and such action would automatically receive the attention of the board and the auditors.

There are occasions when amounts due to outside creditors are also shown in this section, e.g. long-term loans from banks or other third parties. This action gives the appearance of enhancing the net assets whereas, strictly speaking, the amount should have been deducted from the assets in the section of 'creditors of one year or more'. Such entries remain part of the total borrowing of a company and, therefore, affect the gearing ratio. In cases like this the manager should rewrite the balance sheet, putting such entries in their proper place.

Balance sheets – partnership accounts

The asset side of the balance sheet of partnership accounts will be much the same as that for company accounts. However, capital will be represented in a different manner to that of companies (whose situation has just been described). The partnership capital will be shown by stating the amount of capital that each partner had at the beginning of each trading period.

Each partner's proportion of the year's profits (losses) will be added to the capital figure and the drawings deducted from the total. The sum of the net figures is, obviously, the capital of the partnership. However, it should be remembered that the capital amount is gross of tax, i.e. no deduction will ever be made in partnership accounts for income tax. Therefore, when dealing with a partnership the manager needs to enquire whether the tax has been paid to date and to discover the extent to which any tax liability may affect the partnership. Similar considerations apply to the accounts of the sole traders.

Balance sheet and profit and loss account notes

Auditors' notes attached to the accounts form an essential part of those accounts and are a mine of information to a bank manager making an assessment for lending purposes. They need to be read carefully and where they are unclear then the manager needs to have a word with the auditors to clarify the position. If the accounts are going to his head office then the manager can be sure that the lending controller is going to look carefully through them. He should, however, mention any uncertainty when making his report to the controller.

Administration and management charges appearing on profit and loss accounts

Entries regarding these items may be found on the accounts of associated or group companies. Ostensibly, they represent work done by one company on behalf of another, e.g. the bookkeeping of one or more companies may be carried out by another who will make a charge for the service. Similarly, where the directors of one company provide management expertise for one or more other companies then a management charge may be made. However, such charges can be utilised for other purposes as well: they may also be used as a means of transferring profit from one company to another with a view to reducing the immediate corporation tax liability. For example, where one company has made profits but has no capital allowance to set against the profits and another company has unused capital allowances then such a charge may be made in order to get the profit into the company where it would be most advantageous. Corporation tax bands may be used in the same way.

Using administration or management charges in this way of course distorts the structure of the companies concerned and their accounts will not truly represent the various companies' activities. Cash may not pass between the companies as the amount due can be left outstanding on inter-group or associated company accounts or 'hidden' in trade debtors and creditors. None of this is helpful to a bank. However, where it occurs between companies within a group there are few problems for the bank because it will be basing its assessment on the consolidated balance sheet position which excludes all inter-company balances.

Where such charges appear on accounts of associated companies then the manager needs to take a different view entirely. Associated companies will often not have the same balance sheet dates as each other and money can pass between them in a manner which is tax effective for them but which can create a situation where the bank is lending to a company which has had a significant amount of its assets removed by such charges. The only way of lending to such 'groups' of associated companies is to take each one on its merits, to have a limit for each company and to ensure that each company is satisfactorily secured in respect of its own liability.

If this practice of moving funds around continues over several years then obviously the distortions become severe and no bank will be willing to put up funds for the companies involved. This may cause such associated companies to form themselves into a group structure. As far as they are concerned this will not only enable a bank to see their strength in its true light but may well give the directors more strength in the market place generally.

Budgets, management accounts and cash flows

Budgets can include capital and revenue items and should be drawn up before the beginning of each annual trading period to show what the business considers will be its income and expenditure over the ensuing twelve-month period. Management accounts should be drawn up regularly, e.g. monthly or quarterly, and these should show how well the business is performing in relation to its anticipated budget. Cash flows should be drawn up prior to a particular trading period and amended when circumstances dictate that the future cash flow will be significantly altered.

Cash flows are drawn up on a monthly basis and state the expected income during that month. From this an itemised list of revenue and capital expenditure is deducted. The net result of the inflow and outflow of cash during that period is added or deducted from the previous end-of-month bank balance so that the increase or decrease in the bank balance can be shown monthly over any period under consideration. If when drawing up a cash flow, a column is left beside the estimated figures so that the actual figures can be inserted as time goes by then any undue fluctuation in the forecast can be quickly seen. This will provide an early indication that something may be wrong, e.g. that gross profit margins have not been achieved.

The extent to which the manager needs these presentations from his customers is a subjective decision dependent upon the size of the borrowing, the sophistication of the operation and the faith the bank has in the continuing profitability of the business. In calling for documentation of this nature, the manager should be aware that it will take considerable time to prepare and it ought not to be called for unless it is going to be put to good use. However, once a business has progressed beyond a 'sweet shop' economy then it ought to be preparing some documentation along these lines for its own purposes. Indeed the ability to produce such documentation to a good standard will give a bank confidence in the conduct of the business. If a bank insists on seeing such information it can actually be helping the business as the proprietors will undoubtedly gain a better knowledge of the business through the very act of producing what is required. However, often the work has to be carried out by the company's auditors because the proprietors do not have either the time or experience to do it themselves.

Distortions in cash flow

Anyone who has conducted a business will know that however well budgets and cash flows are prepared, it is quite possible that they will be thrown out by the combination of events that affect daily routine. For example, sales and gross profit margins (which are the most difficult to forecast) will vary, as will the costs of purchases; levels of stockholding will alter (perhaps because of the difficulties encountered with suppliers) or a staff problem may give rise to invoices going out late and the amount owed by debtors increasing, thereby reducing the inflow of funds. The manager needs to be aware of the variations which can occur in even a well-run business. He should not, therefore, be surprised to receive a request for a temporary excess over an overdraft limit for a week or so because of a hiccup in a cash flow and should normally meet such a request. But although the customer will be looking for an immediate response this should not deter the manager from deferring a decision for an hour or two if he feels time is needed to consider the matter or to refer it to his lending controller. Where such excesses become more than occasional, it is an indication that the working capital of the company is too low. The manager should therefore consider the possibility of increasing the overdraft limit and also be aware that all may not be well.

Management accounts

Management accounts will be prepared on a monthly basis in a business of any size and are of great value to the bank manager. Their preparation is much easier now that computer accounting systems are available. Such accounts will normally show both the past month's activity in relation to the month's budget and the aggregate situation for the number of months that have passed in the trading period. Table 6.2 is an example of how a monthly management account may look. Looking at this table it can be seen that the business is half-way through its trading year. September was not a good month for sales in relation to the budgeted figure and despite a reduced overhead amount the net profit for the month fell short of the target. However, turning to the year to date, it will be seen that whilst there is a shortfall on sales and on gross profit margin, the final net profit of £68,745 is not too far out from the budgeted figure of £71,136. The evidence indicates that the results are generally in line with expectations.

Nevertheless, there are several matters to be borne in mind when examining such information. Firstly, there is no evidence of any adjustments for stock variations. It may be that the variations in stock have been adjusted by amending the purchases figure and the manager should make enquiries as to the exact position. If the business is one where stock variation is small then the directors may only require a stock-taking every quarter. As this is a quarter day it would be reasonable to expect it to be included. Where there are significant swings in stock valuations, then stock-taking may occur more frequently or management accounts may be adjusted for stock movements by reference to bookkeeping records as opposed to a physical check.

The gross margin percentage is evaluated by taking the mark-up

Table 6.2 An example of a monthly management account

	6th month – September			Year to date			Year
	Budget	Actual		Budget	Actual		Budget
Sales	179,167		168,594	1,075,000		992,133	2,150,000
Purchases	144,489	136,659		866,935	807,785		1,733,871
Direct costs	3,583	11,500		21,500	17,218		43,000
	148,072		148,159	888,435		825,003	1,776,871
Gross profit	31,095		20,435	186,565		167,130	373,129
Gross margin	24.0%		23.4%	24.0%		22.3%	
Overheads	27,426	22,495		164,556	152,537		329,112
Depreciation	1,257	1,257		7,538	7,538		15,075
	28,683		23,752	172,094		160,075	344,187
Net trading profit	2,412		(3,317)	14,471		7,055	28,942
Admin receivable	4,340	4,520		26,040	26,660		52,080
Rebates							
Net discounts	5,104	6,053		30,625	35,030		61,250
			10,573			61,690	
Net profit	11,856		7,256	71,136		68,745	142,272

on purchases to sales and is not the same as the percentage of the gross profit to sales. This is common procedure with a business attempting to obtain a targeted percentage mark-up on the cost of its purchases. Here an average of 24% is targeted and a shortfall of 1.7% is seen for the year to date.

Management account figures should not be regarded as irrefutable. Here, the annual budget totals have been divided by twelve to give the monthly budget figures, which, no doubt, the business finds a satisfactory basis for its general purposes. However, it is unlikely that income or expenditure will fall as neatly into place as that. For example, sales may be more seasonable and it could be that the best selling period has passed or is yet to come. Similarly, overheads appear to be below budget but their accuracy depends on the degree of sophistication brought into the accountancy procedure. It would obviously be unwise to assume that the second six months' trading will produce twice the net profit as shown on the accounts without making enquiries as to the expectations of the business during that period. However, on the whole these are an encouraging set of accounts and, assuming the business is ongoing, they should be quite satisfactory to a banker.

Capital expenditure

The control of capital expenditure assisted by a capital budget is most important. Irrational behaviour occurs in businesses of all sizes and changes of executives can lead to different practices in respect of capital, as well as revenue items. To take a business with an annual turnover of £3,600,000, for example, there will on average be £300,000 received by the company each month and something like the same figure being paid out to creditors, etc. It is not uncommon to find executives knowing that such funds abound concluding that they can spend money on capital items, (e.g. new offices) when in reality the money is not actually there. In the same way, expenditure on such items as additional staff may occur without an appreciation of the consequences of the action – these consequences including calling in of bank advances, loss of employment and possible liquidation, etc.

Bank managers need to be aware that the business world is not necessarily populated with top-class business managers and that many businesses are run by people without formal business management experience who probably came to this kind of management through other career paths. It is in this area that a manager can often help his business customers by guiding them into good routines which will assist customers and bank alike. Whether these are the preparation of budgets, management accounts or cash flows, a bank manager can have a crucial role to play in helping customers realise their potential.

The 'going' concern v. *the 'gone' concern*

As the technical assessment of a 'going' concern and a 'gone' concern features prominently in all bank training programmes relating to balance sheets and profit and loss accounts, the subject will not be discussed here in any depth. All that need be said here is that the two categories used when assessing a business in relation to the bank are the 'going' concern, i.e. the amount a business is worth where the concern is trading satisfactorily, and the 'gone' concern, i.e. the value of the business if it fails. Under the latter the value of the assets of a business will be slashed to produce a figure which the bank roughly expects will be realised by a liquidator. It is important for the manager to keep these different assessments in perspective and, particularly, not to let the 'gone' position outweigh the 'going' position in cases where there is no cause for fear about the company continuing on a profitable basis or doubt about the ability of those conducting it. A certain level of caution is obviously important but industry and commerce are risk-taking areas and banks have to support good customers in their endeavours to increase business. Businessmen have to take a long-term view about the future of their business and the introduction of new products and ideas. Indeed when assessing new business customers a manager should ask about the strength of the business in the market place and the resources being put into fresh objectives or products. Whilst a banker should always establish that there is a sound source of repayment or security to fall back upon, too much attention to the 'gone' factor can have an unduly inhibiting effect. Once again, the manager's ability to correctly assess a business is all important.

For example, a well-run limited company is seeking an advance for a purpose within the company's normal objectives. It proposes to secure the loan by a floating charge but without any other security. The limit is 35% below the normal level of debtors but the 'gone' assessment reveals that upon liquidation the company would only pay 75 pence in the pound. Thus the bank has a customer who is trading satisfactorily, who requires funds for an acceptable purpose and whose 'going' source of repayment looks justifiable. It would be quite wrong to decline this advance because the 'gone' position was not entirely satisfactory, especially when in the event of the bank having to appoint a receiver the debtors alone would cover the amount of the advance. There is every reason in these circumstances to suppose that the bank would be repaid. This is admittedly a rather simple demonstration of the relationship between the 'going' and the 'gone' positions and one which ignores preferential creditors. However, it does serve to show the need to keep the two separate assessments in balance so that the manager does not inhibit the expansion of his own business and that of his customers through over-cautiousness.

REPAYMENT – GENERAL

This subject has already been dealt with to some extent under the sub-headings of Gearing, Balance sheet and profit and loss accounts, Budgets, Management accounts and Cash flows and the 'Going' and 'Gone' concern aspects through which the repayment of a bank advance may be assessed. However, to turn briefly again to our new manager at Barretts bank in Millchester on his first day, how is he to get to grips with the practical business of assessment? It has already been suggested that he used the mnemonic 'MARS-Cost' as an *aide mémoire* and such a practice will help him acquire the necessary information without wasting too much time. Providing he can explain why he needs this, he should have no difficulty in persuading reluctant customers to produce the accounts and internal control documentation he requires in order to assess their capability. The standard of presentation of such information and whether the manager feels matters are being hidden from the bank's view will both be critical favours in this assessment. The manager is entitled to expect complete frankness from the customers and an atmosphere of mutual trust. These will form a good background to the manager's task of getting to the financial heart of a customer's business.

Security

The security aspect of lending to business borrowers is dealt with fully in Chapter 7 and does not need any specific explanation at this point.

Interest, charges and arrangement fees

It is essential at the negotiating stage of an advance that the bank's remuneration be discussed so that the customer can agree a satisfactory income level with the manager. Customers will be expecting the price for the service to be arranged then and will be more receptive to the discussion at this stage than if it is left to a later date (see also 'Interests and charges' in Chapter 4).

The manager will obviously seek a level of charges and interest in accordance with bank policy. However, although he will usually be able to obtain this he may be faced with circumstances where a customer has been charged on the low side in the past. Alternatively, the manager may be attempting to obtain fresh business for the bank in a competitive situation. The latter is acceptable practice as long as the charging level can be justified. Managers must, without showing 'favour', have the freedom to vary costs according to circumstances.

The application of charges will also be in accordance with the bank practice and is normally quarterly. Quite frequently the debiting of charges to an account takes it over the limit and business accounts should be allowed a little while to digest this debit. (Although in theory they should have allowed for the debit, in practice it is only when the entry appears on the bank statement that many businesses take charges into account.) A bank is under no compulsion to advise customers in advance of charges but the manager may feel that with certain accounts advice should be given immediately after the posting occurs. Business invoices normally get paid in the first week of any month. Consequently, any excess caused by debiting charges to a bank account ought to be repaid during that period. Failure to do so is a sign of weakness in an account.

Fees for arranging an advance will normally be taken once the loan has been drawn or following the customer's agreement to a borrowing facility. Sometimes it is agreed that they should be taken at the end of the current charging period, in which cases it is necessary to ensure that an adequate recording system exists so that the charge is not overlooked. Whilst the standard tariff will cover most normal activity on the account, sometimes the manager or other members of the staff become involved in work on behalf of the customer which is more time-consuming and for which a higher charge should be made. Managers, for instance, may be involved in lengthy discussions with customers concerning disposal and acquisition of assets, mergers, premises, etc. In any other profession such advice would have to be paid for on a time basis. There is no reason why a bank manager should not cost his time in a similar way and add that to the periodic bank charge. Quite often customers fail to raise the subject of the cost of borrowing because they are more concerned with the need to obtain finance. The matter should not be left to rest and in such cases the manager must introduce the subject himself.

Memorandum and Articles of Association

When lending to a company managers must study the company's Memorandum to ensure that it permits the company to carry out the business for which the advance is required and that the borrowing is within the powers of the company. A non-trading company has no power to borrow unless its Memorandum gives permission to do so. If borrowing which is beyond the legal power (*ultra vires*) of the company is permitted, then the company effectively has no liability for the debt. Although there are certain ways for a bank to protect itself in such a position (including relying on the European Communities Act 1972) reading the Memorandum of the company will put the matter beyond doubt from the outset.

Similarly, the powers of the directors to borrow money on behalf of the company are set out in the Articles of Association and these powers may be unlimited or restricted to stated levels. If there is a restriction on the level of borrowing then the bank must ensure that such a level is not exceeded – in order to prevent the borrowing being *ultra vires* the directors. In the unfortunate event of a bank finding itself in a position of being *ultra vires* the directors, the best remedy is to ask the directors to call a general meeting of the company. At this meeting a resolution should be passed ratifying the excess borrowing. Providing the borrowing is within the powers given the company in its Memorandum, it is quite legal to follow this procedure.

It is probably true to say that today the large majority of private limited companies and their directors have unlimited powers of borrowing. However, managers must not let this be an excuse for becoming lax in this area and they should still ensure that attention is paid to Memorandum and Articles of Association prior to making an advance.

Applications to a head office regarding the provision of funds

Where managers wish to make an advance in excess of their discretionary limits then they will follow the normal bank procedure of submitting a proposal for the advance to their lending controller. This subject is dealt with in detail in the section on 'The lending controller' in Chapter 3 and the section 'Documentation and advising' in Chapter 4.

START-UP FINANCE

From the banking point of view start-up finance is defined as an application for an advance the purpose of which is to provide funds in order that a customer may undertake a new business venture. It is an area of high banking risk and the advice which a bank manager needs when asked to put up such funds is perhaps the same as that given by Mr Punch to a couple about to get married i.e. 'don't'!

Proposals of this nature fall into categories, of varying degrees of difficulty:

1. one or more customers propose to start up a business in which they have no previous experience;
2. one or more customers intend to start up a business in an area in which they are experienced but they have not traded as a business before;
3. customers with an established business wish to start up or acquire a business in a different area to their existing trade and one in which they have no prior experience.

Although there are other permutations on these themes, the three situations above will suffice in this context as definitions of cases where start-up finance is commonly required.

The first two examples are dealt with in the 'Question and Answer' below. The third example will possibly produce proposals more likely to be acceptable to a bank. These will probably involve a customer who has a good trading record and who wishes to move into a new venture but who only intends to make an investment which will not seriously upset his trading base if the venture fails. In such a start-up where the investment is substantial, perhaps needing assets similar to those of the existing business, then there is a danger that if the venture fails the established business will be brought down with it. A lending assessment in this case will therefore be conditioned by the degree of the customer's involvement in his new business in relation to his involvement with the existing business. The example which follows, illustrating the situations described in categories 1 and 2 above, is a typical request for start-up finance from two respectable people who have carefully considered giving up their employment and starting a business of their own. The answer to the problem highlights the difficulties that the branch manager will encounter. With a little imagination, it can be seen how much easier it is to assess a request for an advance from an existing business.

Question

A branch manager interviews a Mr Pepper and a Mr Howard, both in their mid-thirties. Mr Pepper was known to the bank through his personal account, where he was described as a sales director of a manufacturing company, and Mr Howard is introduced as being a production engineer in the same company. They explain to the manager that for a long time they have wanted to set up in business on their own, that they have now discovered an area in which they believe there is good market potential and that they have a product which can be manufactured on a small capital base. They believe that a total capital of £40,000 will be needed, of which they already have £15,000 themselves. They have come to explore the possibilities of the bank providing £25,000 towards the venture. They have prepared documentation and want the manager to advise them generally on the sort of difficulties they might encounter. This type of situation occurs regularly. Why is a lender faced with a problem when confronted with such a request?

Answer/assessment

It is natural that people wishing to set up in business should approach their local branch bank to see what assistance can be given. Certainly, any bank would be interested in discussing what involvement the bank could have. However, from a lending point of view, considerable difficulties are presented by the fact that no trading record yet exists for the venture that is proposed.

If the bank decides that it can help, a great deal will have to be taken on trust – many ventures of this sort fail. The manager has to satisfy himself that there is going to be an adequate demand for the product and that the business will be able to produce its product to the right quality, in the right packaging and at the right price, etc. It is a high-risk situation and really requires risk capital to start up, rather than a normal bank overdraft/loan. The capital level as stated is, on standard formulas, too low compared with the amount of bank participation requested. Furthermore, it is difficult to determine with certainty the source of repayment and the ability to meet interest payments.

If Mr Pepper and Mr Howard are capable of running a business it is probable that they will have an estimated cash flow and budget for their first twelve months of trading amongst their documentation. The existence of these forecasts and the standard to which they have been prepared may well give the manager some indication as to whether or not the business is sufficiently professional for the venture to succeed. However, the manager will also know that even if a great deal of thought has been put into the forecasts, it is a fortunate new business that manages to keep to its figures. It may also be difficult for the bank to know whether or not the figures are accurate, especially the sales forecast and whether the requested limit is accurate. Indeed, it is probably wise to recognise that even if the business gets off to a good start it may have to come back to the bank for additional funds.

Mr Pepper and Mr Howard will probably be thinking of forming a limited company but they will effectively be working as a partnership. The manager will wonder how they are going to get on together. The success of the business will depend upon their ability to co-operate with one another and face up to problems together. They will also have to be able to conduct a business in its entirety in contrast to the situation hitherto where they have only been responsible for one aspect. They are also entering a different area from that in which they are already experienced. They may well be married which may mean diverting funds which would otherwise be used for expansion. It is a good idea to find out whether in fact both men need to be employed from the outset as to employ only one would keep this aspect of expenditure down.

In such circumstances, the bank will obviously want to discuss the possibility of security. In this situation the question requires a somewhat different approach to that used when considering an advance to a trading operation already in existence. In the latter case a satisfactory source of profit and repayment can be established, whereas in the former such information is not available. The bank would normally look to security as a last resort and generally would not lend if there were reason to believe that the bank would have to rely on it from the outset. Frequently all that is offered in a business situation such as this is a second mortgage over the residential properties of the partners. The problems in realising the security in such circumstances are obvious, despite what may be said at the outset. If a more realistic security is offered then it will enhance the proposition. However, consideration should also be given to realising free assets at the time the business is formed, thus freeing the early profits from interest or funding charges. There is little doubt that the bank would need to give a moratorium in respect of any loan repayments, for it will be unusual for adequate profits to be available in the early stages.

Because of the difficulties that surround start-up finance the use of equity participation or Government Loan Guarantee schemes could well be considered. However, equity participation in banking terms would normally only be available to an established business which needed to expand its share capital base. Furthermore, the same questions as the bank raises will be asked when the funds are requested for a start-up with equity participation. The Government Loan Guarantee Scheme offers another source of money where, given agreement, the Government would cover 80% of the borrowed funds. The bank, however, would have to confirm to the Department of Trade and Industry that it would have been quite happy to lend the funds were it not for the absence of security. Individual circumstances will dictate whether or not the bank feels able to make such a statement.

Therefore, to summarise, a proposition such as that made by Mr Pepper and Mr Howard is unlikely to be acceptable under normal lending criteria. While most banks can relate stories of famous and successful customers who have always been grateful for being lent a small sum of money against the odds when they first started, there are many more cases where money has been lent and lost. Requests for start-up finance usually defy the principles of bank lending and the funds required are high risk money more appropriately supplied by way of equity participation. Those who supply equity finance take considerable trouble and, therefore, time (often months) in investigating the intended business. A bank manager rarely has the time to investigate such proposals thoroughly at the outset and sometimes lacks the experience to do so. Nevertheless there will be occasions when it is felt reasonable to support such a proposition and then the security should be watertight. The manager will be lucky if 20% of those start-ups which he decides to finance are reasonably successful. He would be well advised to keep the number of accounts in this category to a minimum.

CHEQUES DRAWN IN EXCESS OF OVERDRAFT LIMITS

Much of what needs to be said on this subject has already been stated under 'Dishonour' in Chapter 4 and 'Paying cheques' in Chapter 5. All that needs stressing here is that while it is essential that overdraft limits are held in respect by customers, it is a particularly serious matter to dishonour a business customer's cheque. It is suggested that managers need not show immediate concern over occasional trivial – say 10% over the limit – excesses, especially if the borrowing is secured. If the telephone is immediately resorted to over a small excess the confidence of the customer may well be lost. However, if the excesses continue regularly then the limit is clearly too low for the undertaking and the customer should be invited to rethink the matter with the manager.

The successful credit control of temporary excesses is a skill which must be cultivated. The lending controller, on the one hand, expects to see a limited number of excesses in any branch and the manager, on the other hand, has to respond to the trading situations of his customers. A new manager needs to avoid the dangers of both becoming over-anxious in this area or of accepting unsupported stories from customers. When it comes to large excesses it is necessary to telephone and advise the customer of the situation on the account. Whether the cheques are paid or not will depend on the manager's opinion of the response he receives to his news and whether the additional borrowing can be secured. The bank is committed to a limit and there is no reason why this should be exceeded without prior discussion. The manager will be held responsible for any cheques that are paid and he should always consult the lending controller in cases of doubt.

SUMMARY

The correct relationship between banker and customer is one of partnership, with both partners being able to speak frankly to one another. However, by now it should have become clear that the advancing of money to business account customers is not an area for an over-sympathetic, soft approach. Every thought should be given to a business customer's needs, but in the end the overriding consideration must be whether this particular lending is good for the bank. It is not easy to establish that a current account will work satisfactorily when granted an overdraft limit or that a loan will be repaid regularly and on time. However, managers who ensure that they have all the information available about a proposition will be in a strong position when agreeing to lend. Above all, it is vital that the entrepreneurial skill of a business borrower be evaluated. Managers should never forget that customers must be fully competent in the kind and level of business in which they propose to be engaged if their objectives are to be achieved.

CHAPTER 7

Security

'Nothing astonishes men so much as common sense and plain speaking'
Essays 1841, First series (Art), R. W. Emerson

Only a very few accounts are sufficiently creditworthy to warrant unsecured facilities. However, the amount lent to those few accounts as do exist in this category is often substantial and forms a significant amount of a bank's lending business because the majority of such accounts will be large public companies with immense resources and with a remote chance of failure. By no means all public companies are in this situation and many of them will give security to a bank either by direct charge or through a floating charge. In most instances, therefore, it is true to say that a bank requires security in one form or another.

The idea of security is a perfectly logical one: if the source of repayment fails then the bank will sell the security and obtain repayment through the proceeds. Any lender, banker or otherwise, would obviously be foolish to enter into a transaction without ensuring that there is ultimately a source of repayment. Furthermore, the quality of the security is all important. An acceptable security should be capable of valuation and be saleable, realisable and easy to transfer or mortgage. This means that the person to whom the security has been given should be able to obtain a good title to it as well as sell it without difficulty.

CASH

Cash is naturally the best form of security that can be obtained and is frequently the kind which is offered. If the cash being put up as security belongs to the borrower then it is appropriate to write a letter saying that the bank is treating the deposit as security for the relevant limit, i.e. indicating that the money is set-off. Where the amount involved is large or where the money has been deposited by a third party to secure the customer's account then the bank should take a letter of hypothecation (lien) which indicates that the credit balance may not be reduced below a stated figure and that the bank is allowed to combine the amounts without notice.

BEARER BONDS

Where available and of a satisfactory value, these are an excellent form of security because the deposit of such bonds coupled with a Memorandum of Deposit will give the bank a good title. They are also capable of being sold without a customer's assistance. The branch will need to pay careful attention to the cutting of the coupons at the right time by having entries in the branch bearer bond/coupon diary. The manager's second-in-command should be instructed to ensure that this is kept under review.

LIFE POLICIES

Again, these are excellent security up to the surrender value that is attached to them. Policies without a surrender value, be they endowment, whole life or term assurance, are only of value in the sense that they will provide funds in the event of the insured's death. Where a business depends upon a principal director or partner it is in the interest of the bank to secure term assurance so that it can be fully repaid in the event of the insured's death. This will also protect the family of the person insured, especially where a personal asset has been charged to secure a business account.

Life policies drawn in favour of beneficiaries other than the customer who is the insured, will need careful attention. This is because any third party involved in a policy will have to sign the assignment of the policy. The third party should be specifically named, e.g. the insured's husband or wife should be described by name and should not be referred to as 'my wife/husband'. This is because a policy which does not specifically designate by name is ambiguous. For example, when a bank needs to rely on the policy, it may find that the wife or husband referred to at the time of execution of the assignment may have predeceased or divorced the beneficiary and a second spouse has taken his/her place. Any policy without a specifically designated beneficiary is unlikely to be acceptable. However, it may be possible to alter the name of the beneficiary by deed.

STOCKS AND SHARES

Government securities and any stock or share quoted upon The Stock Exchange come under this heading. They are good security because they are easy to value and to charge and are quickly realised if the customer is unable to repay the advance. The value of the shares will not normally fluctuate in a way which works against the bank, provided a reasonable margin is taken at the outset.

A reasonable margin would be 10% on gilt-edged securities, 20% on good commercial shares and 33% on speculative investments, e.g. mining shares. When there is a period of recession on The Stock Exchange, a frequent revaluation of the shares should be carried out, particularly when margins are tight – possibly daily. Where the position alters so that the advance is no longer covered the customer must be asked to deposit fresh security or to make other satisfactory arrangements with the bank.

It is possible to take an equitable or legal charge over Government securities and shares. Usually, banks are satisfied with an equitable charge supported by the execution of a blank common transfer form which enables the bank to sell without reference to the customer or without needing his assistance. If a legal charge is taken then the shares will be transferred into the name of a bank nominee company so that there is an actual transfer of ownership and dividends will be paid to the nominee company instead of direct to the shareholder. The nominee company will pass the dividend money to the bank account of the customer at the relevant times. Where a bank is satisfied that the name on the certificate is that of its customer and that there is no doubt that the customer is the true beneficial owner of the holding then an equitable charge is acceptable security. If there is insufficient evidence for the manager to be satisfied that the depositor of the stocks or shares is the beneficial owner than a legal charge ought to be taken. For example, occasionally a manager may decide to lend to a new customer on the security of shares even though the customer is previously unknown. In these cases the manager should consider proceeding to a legal mortgage in order to obtain protection from any prior rights, e.g. a trust which could upset an equitable charge if one were to be taken.

No value can be placed on unquoted shares – which are normally those of private companies – because of the difficulty of realising them in case of need. It would almost certainly be difficult to find a buyer. There are normally restrictions within the company's Memorandum and Articles of Association preventing the free transfer of its shares and ensuring that they are offered to the existing shareholders first. This would prevent any other willing purchaser being able to acquire them. If a charge is taken over them they should be generally regarded as valueless, although they might produce something in the event of non-repayment of an advance. They may be charged for control purposes rather than for any value.

NATIONAL SAVINGS CERTIFICATES AND PREMIUM SAVINGS BONDS

These investments have some of the qualities of stocks and shares in that they have a readily quantifiable value and are easy to realise. However, they suffer from a weakness in that in the event of being lost, duplicates can be issued to the owner and can be encashed. If a Memorandum of Deposit is taken over them, it needs to be supported by an undated encashment form. However, such security should only be taken from customers who are regarded as respectable. The vast majority of bank customers can be regarded as such and lending against National Savings Certificates and Premium Bonds frequently occurs on a satisfactory basis for small amounts.

LAND

Today, land (and all that stands upon it) forms the largest part of the total security taken by the average bank. It may be difficult to imagine that there was a time when taking a mortgage over deeds was frowned upon in banking. Furthermore, although second mortgages form a significant part of the private account security portfolio nowadays, they only really became acceptable around 1960. Taking a charge over land is something with which managers will be well accustomed on reaching their first managerial appointment and it presents no special difficulties other than the need to ensure that all parties who may have an interest in the property concerned join in the charge or assent to it. The fact that the law has conferred rights on common law wives, children and others who have made a contribution to a property, or in some other way have given the owner benefit, has made it more difficult to ensure that a bank has a good title where such circumstances exist. Therefore, when charging residential property, enquiries do need to be made on each occasion as to the existence of any non-apparent rights. Where they are found to exist suitable steps need to be taken in accordance with bank regulations. There should be no hesitation in asking questions on this matter although some customers may be surprised or offended by such enquiries. Obviously, in such circumstances a tactful approach will be especially necessary.

Whilst freehold and long leasehold properties present little problem to a lending manager, he will need to be very wary about taking charges over short leases, i.e. twenty-one years and under, which are commonly rental agreements in respect of shops or offices. There may occasionally be some value in such a lease where the rental is below the economic rent. However, even in those circumstances there is rarely any real value in such leases since at the end of the agreed period the lessor will undoubtedly negotiate an economic rent which will remove any value from the lease. Furthermore, all such leases will contain a bankruptcy clause, the effect of which is to allow the freeholder into possession if rent falls into arrears. The bankruptcy clause will take precedence over any bank charge. Any leases which are reaching the end of their term may involve the leaseholder in costly dilapidations – a feature to be borne in mind when discussing this sort of security with customers.

Property valuation

It has been established that there should be a realistic valuation of any property which is to be charged to the bank. It is therefore essential that, prior to agreeing to an advance, any property to be taken as security should be inspected by the manager. The only exception to this rule is probably where there is a 'bridging' advance when both the vendor's and the purchaser's sale contracts are being exchanged simultaneously. The manager may well be able to place a valuation on residential property by an exterior inspection in which the condition of the property, the type of neighbourhood in which it stands and the structure should all be considered. The valuation must assess the likelihood of an easy sale should the need arise. Where houses are screened by trees or other buildings or the manager feels that it is necessary to go inside to carry out a full inspection then arrangements should be made with the customer for this purpose. All valuations must be conservative and based on existing conditions, not those which the customer believes will obtain at a later date, e.g. through planning permission. The manager should bear in mind that a customer may place too high a valuation on his house and where a dispute arises because the bank's valuation is much lower than the customer's a professional valuation should be obtained.

It is customary in normal lending to advance up to roughly 70% of the value of the property where the latter is being used as security. However, with house mortgage lending, this figure may well be increased to a higher level in accordance with the regulations laid down by the bank. There will be times when the manager is asked to exceed the standard lending margin. In these circumstances, he will have to decide whether or not this can be justified by the value of the property being offered. There will be instances when a manager feels unable to assess a property because of its unique position, its size or some factor which is out of his range of experience. In these circumstances, he should employ a professional valuer to inspect the property at the customer's expense.

Office and industrial premises

Assessment of office and industrial premises requires more expertise on the part of the manager than does residential property. A newly appointed manager will do well to acquaint himself with the general method of such valuations if he has not learnt them already, and should make it his business to discover the level of rents being paid for industrial and office premises in the district. A working knowledge should also be acquired of the percentage return that an investor would be willing to accept on the purchase price should he wish to buy an industrial or office property. For example, if the going rent for 20,000 square feet of office accommodation is £8 per square foot then the annual rental for the office building will be £160,000 per annum. Where the general economic climate and condition and position of the property is such that a purchaser of the freehold would be looking for a 10% return on the investment, then the value of the property will be £1,600,000. This is an over-simplification of valuation methods and the percentage return will often vary considerably according to the position and size of the property – possibly spanning from 4% to 15% or even higher.

Branch managers can obtain information in this area from estate agents and valuers, who will often be willing to discuss the property market with them. The branch's existing experience of dealing with property together with information about property transactions which appear in local newspapers are the elements which the manager can use to establish a working knowledge in this field. Managers are not expected to become experts in property valuation, although many of them do. All they need to learn is how to form a useful opinion about the value of a property and to recognise at what point a qualified valuer's opinion is needed. Such a valuation may well enable the bank to advance a somewhat higher sum against the property than would otherwise have been the case.

The valuation of industrial and office property is another instance where a manager will need to use his own initiative in order to gain sufficient knowledge to make accurate assessments. It is important that the basic skills are acquired in order to converse ably with customers. The margin taken against the valuation of this type of property may be between 50% and 60%.

Planning

Local searches in respect of planning permissions are always obtained before advances are made against the security of the property and the results of such searches will obviously affect any value that is placed upon the property. There are times when managers will be asked to lend funds in anticipation of planning permission being obtained, where such planning permission may considerably enhance the value of land, e.g. where the building of residential properties on previously undeveloped land is permitted. It must be stressed that no account should be taken of any such potential value until planning permission has actually come through. This may sound a fairly obvious precaution but it has not always been observed – to the cost of both bank and customer.

During the property boom in the 1970s, there were many instances where customers persuaded banks to advance money well above the existing-use value on land awaiting planning permission. The value of the land as security at the time of the advance was therefore well below the amount lent. Subsequently, planning permission was not given and the bank was left with a loan advanced against relatively worthless security. Both customers and bank paid for these errors in judgement. Managers need to remember in the midst of a property boom that the boom will not last forever. Indeed, such situations are times when it is particularly important to ensure that sound principles concerning lending in respect of property are followed.

Certain types of planning permissions in respect of industrial premises place conditions upon the disposal of properties by owners. For example, the local council may decide that it wishes to encourage local industry rather than outside industry and may place a condition on a property which insists that in the event of a sale purchasers must come from a defined locality. Such a condition obviously restricts the marketability of a property and therefore lowers its value. In the event of a customer receiving a planning permission along those lines, he should be encouraged to appeal. The existence of such conditions will not only reduce the bank's ability to assist him but will also present long-term problems in the event of his wishing to move at a later date.

Insurance

When accepting property as security the bank will require evidence of fire insurance and of the payment of the annual premium. They will also want proof that the insurance company has noted bank interest in the policy in their books. In the longer term, the manager will need to make certain that insurance cover keeps pace with any inflationary value of the building. This check applies to all customers' insurance policies in which the bank has an interest in general – be it cover over stocks, loss of profits, plant and machinery or any other asset where a bank could be significantly affected by an insurable loss. With businesses of any size, there is likely to be a comprehensive policy covering the whole range of insured assets. The branch should have a copy of this and, if need be, hold permission to discuss the terms of the insurance with the customer's insurance broker from time to time.

GUARANTEES AND INDEMNITIES

The essential practical point to be remembered in respect of guarantees and indemnities is that they are a weak security and, generally speaking, should not be relied upon to produce funds in case of need. There are, of course, times when wealthy guarantors giving guarantees for relatively small amounts may be satisfactory, especially where the source of repayment is good. However, on the whole, the manager must remember that a guarantee is only an undertaking to pay if the principal debtor defaults. Should that situation arise a bank will have to start the process of persuading the guarantor to part with the funds that are rightfully due to it. In many cases, a guarantor called upon to meet a liability will demur and try to avoid it by offering to pay by instalments; seek to do a deal suggesting that the bank settles for part of the amount due; or refuse to pay altogether. This leaves the bank the unattractive option of suing for the money. It is therefore clear that in practice seeking repayment of a liability through an unsupported guarantee can often be difficult and unrewarding; an unsupported guarantee (or indemnity) can be one of the weakest forms of security available – indeed in some quarters it is scarcely regarded as security at all.

Where a guarantee is supported by tangible security then the bank can have recourse to security if the guarantor is unable to find funds from other sources. In those cases the security will be as good as a straightforward charge over the particular asset that lies in support, up to any limit expressed in the guarantee. Managers should not feel, however, that guarantees should never taken. Their existence can ensure repayment from a source other than through the guarantees and, of course, there are guarantors who do honour their liabilities.

Guarantees from company directors

When lending to a private company of modest size, it is expedient to insist upon directors' guarantees in support (unless there is a strong tangible security situation). This is because if the company's business is ailing at any time the board may well be more influenced towards ensuring that the advance is repaid if faced with the prospect of being sued under the guarantees if it is not.

It is hardly surprising that directors often object to executing personal guarantees and do not wish to tie their private monies to that of the business. In the same way, they may well object to guaranteeing the lease of business premises when asked to do so by the lessor. It is a very natural reaction for a company director to be unwilling to enter into guarantees, and in these circumstances the manager must simply make his mind up whether he is going to insist upon having the guarantees – and if he is then no funds should be provided until they are executed. Whilst acknowledging the directors' concern, the manager could well point out that private limited companies exist for the personal benefit of the directors and that directors ought not to be able to hide their private assets behind limited liability when seeking advances which are ultimately to their personal benefit.

Execution of guarantees

The execution of guarantees needs special care and there are many textbooks full of advice on the technical aspects of the matter. The branch manager cannot be too cautious when taking a guarantee and he is best advised to ensure that he meets the customer and the proposed guarantor for a discussion. He should have his customer's permission to speak freely to the guarantor with a view to ensuring that both understand the liability being proposed and the potential likelihood or otherwise of the guarantor being called upon to meet his liability. It is important that an interview note is subsequently made recording these discussions. There may be times when it is in the bank's interests for the manager to write to the guarantor briefly stating the agreement into which the bank is proposing to enter, making certain that the letter is written without prejudice to the guarantee document itself.

There are many occasions when guarantees can be properly signed in the manager's office in accordance with the bank's regulations and the bank then obtains an enforceable document. Nevertheless, in order to protect the bank to the greatest degree wherever possible the manager should insist that the guarantees be signed by the guarantor at the offices of an independent solicitor (not the bank's solicitor) who will explain the purport of the document. This applies to male and female guarantors (guarantrixes) and no distinction should be made between them. Where a person executing a guarantee can clearly be seen to be wholly conversant with the liability it may not be necessary to obtain a solicitor's presence when executing the guarantee.

Guarantees from limited companies

Guarantees (indemnities) to be taken from a limited company will require an investigation of that company's financial standing in the same way as if a bank were considering an application from the proposed guarantor for an advance. If the company should be wound-up then the guarantee will probably be worthless. The directors of a company faced with a liability under a guarantee to a bank may be able to run the company down, e.g. by transferring its trade to another company, thereby leaving the bank in an awkward position. This practice has been successfully used from time to time by unscrupulous directors and those attempting fraud.

Default

In the event of a customer defaulting and formal demand being made it will be necessary to make formal demand upon any guarantors or depositors of third party securities at the same time. This does not usually mean that a bank will see fit to pursue third parties immediately, for it will wish to obtain redress from the customer's free assets or by realising any direct security first. If necessary it may subsequently proceed against the depositors of third party security for the balance of the funds outstanding to the bank.

DEBENTURES, FLOATING CHARGES AND CHARGES OVER COMPANY BOOK DEBTS

These securities suffer from the same defect as guarantees, in that they are difficult to value in respect of the sum that may be available if a bank finds it necessary to appoint a receiver – which power is given to a bank in each of those particular forms of charge. Prior to taking one of these securities, a manager should have assessed from audited accounts on a 'gone' basis the worth of the company giving the charge, i.e. what its value would be if the business was in the course of being wound-up. This will produce a figure which should, theoretically, be sufficient to cover the proposed advance if it were sanctioned. However, unless a dramatic mistake has been made, the borrowing will probably not be called in for at least the next year or two and, during that time, significant changes may have occurred in the company's accounts which have created a worse situation than could have been anticipated. Therefore, if one of these charges is to be taken without the support of adequate tangible security, the manager should ensure that the company is in a strong position at the outset.

Various trading factors can upset the bank's assessment of a company which has reached the point where it can no longer trade. Chief of these will be the increase in the amount owing to preferential creditors. When a company's finances come under pressure, the directors tend to meet their trade creditors and pay wages in order to keep the company in business. As a result, payments to preferential creditors, e.g. PAYE, National Insurance and VAT, may well fall into arrears and by the time the bank appoints a receiver the total amount in front of the bank advance can be so substantial that the charge becomes valueless.

Receivers' fees

An important point to recall is that the appointment of a receiver is an expensive business. He is the agent of the bank and whilst he is entitled to recoup his fees from the assets of the company, if those assets are insufficient it will be the bank who will have to pay the balance. A receiver's fees for quite a small company could well amount to £4,000 to £5,000 and it would not have to be a company of great size before the fees reached £15,000 or more. The lending controller of the bank needs to take this aspect into account before agreeing to the appointment of a receiver.

The value to a bank

It follows that securities such as debentures, floating charges and charges over company book debts are only valuable to a bank in securing the advances of medium to large companies. At that level they can often be taken without any other support. For example, if a company has trade debtors of £500,000 with an overdraft limit of £100,000 then it is prima facie reasonable to suppose that the bank's position would be covered in the event of having to appoint a receiver and that he would be able to obtain sufficient to repay the overdraft, any accrued interest and his fee.

When considering these securities in relation to small companies, the position is entirely different. There can be a temptation for managers keen to support a company which appears to have a reasonable future but where there is no tangible security to take a floating charge, supported by the personal guarantees of the directors of limited means, and to convince themselves that such a security will cover the advance. One or two advances made on this basis may be satisfactorily concluded and this might induce a sense of false security when it comes to considering a further similar application. What should be recognised is that the initial one or two advances, although repaid, were never sound lending propositions and if difficulties had arisen there would have been nothing to fall back upon. It only requires one such account to turn bad for the bank to lose more than the sum earned in the others – and it is quite likely that such a situation could occur.

This situation can be demonstrated by looking at two examples. Firstly, assume that Figure 7.1 shows the position of a company under a floating charge where there is no other security which approaches the bank and asks them to appoint a receiver or where the bank has called a halt itself and made formal demand.

The bank will have no option but to appoint a receiver with £70,000 outstanding and £120,000 of assets available to it under its charge. It may hope to get, say, £40,000 from the debtors and the balance from stock. However, the latter, on a forced sale basis, may yield considerably less than the directors' valuation. Moreover, amongst the £100,000 creditors, there will be an amount due in respect of preferential creditors which could easily have reached as

Fig. 7.1 Company A

	Company A		
Creditors	£100,000	Debtors	£50,000
Overdraft	70,000	Stock (at directors' valuation)	70,000
	£170,000		£120,000

much as £20,000. The receiver's fees will also make further inroads into the gross amount to be raised from the assets. In such circumstances it is by no means certain that the bank will receive full repayment.

If we take another set of figures which are a tenth of the size of the previous company, the position is as shown in Figure 7.2 for company B.

Fig. 7.2 Company B

	Company B		
Creditors	£10,000	Debtors	£5,000
Overdraft	7,000	Stock	7,000
	£17,000		£12,000

This company presents all the same problems to the bank as the one in the first example did, as well as the added problem that the receiver's fees are likely to be disproportionately high in relation to the amount of the company's assets or the bank overdraft. Possibly the bank might have to consider adding as much as £4,000 in respect of fees to the overdraft of £7,000 and would hope to get £11,000 from the total assets of £12,000 after payment of preferential creditors. It is quite likely that from a little business such as this one no more than £7,000 would be obtained out of current assets. Bearing in mind preferentials, an appointment of a receiver is probably unacceptable and the bank will have to rely on what the liquidator produces.

The second example illustrates the inadvisability of relying on a floating charge from small companies: once they get into difficulties there is often insufficient money left to make any action by the bank worthwhile. There is the possibility that, given the ability to appoint a receiver purely in respect of the debtors, a more economic operation could be mounted. This would depend on the facts of the matter in question.

There is an old Greek proverb which runs 'when the tree is fallen, all go with their hatchet'. A good illustration of this can be seen in Figure 7.3, which is the Statement of Affairs of a limited company together with notes relating to the winding-up of it.

Although the bank was only owed £4,093, it can be seen that the assets have been swallowed up by the company's landlord, the preferential creditors and by a factoring company deducting £28,425 from the funds it was collecting from trade debtors. The possibility of seizure of assets by a landlord in distraint for arrears of rent is not something lenders always consider. Assets totalling £19,588 were seized to satisfy rent of £7,713. The fact that these assets won't actually realise anything for the creditors shows how wary one needs to be about the value of assets. As there is insufficient money to satisfy the preferential creditors, the bank will not receive any money to pay off the advance. The debt will have to be written off even though it is secured by a debenture. The factoring company has, of course, recovered its advances. It should also be noted that the net trade debtors of £33,323 are only anticipated to realise £12,000 – which is a considerably lower figure than might normally be expected. Note 4 indicates the type of problem faced by a liquidator who lacks the resources necessary to enable him to pursue actions to the benefit of creditors. Note 5 acts as a further reminder that what may appear to be a company asset may only actually be leased and of no value to a bank.

Another example of the fall in value of assets (and of an absence of managerial efficiency) can be seen in the report of the liquidator dealing with Walter Howard Designs Ltd made in February 1986. This company had £1.3 million of unpaid creditors as well as a further £1.4 million of issued capital. The report stated, *inter alia*:

> 'On the information available at present the Official Receiver is of the opinion that the failure and insolvency of the company is primarily attributable to its directors in that they caused the company's business to become dependent on a small number of customers and thereby left the company without the financial resources needed to adapt to a changing pattern of trade; it would appear, however, that a substantial part of the deficiency is attributable to the loss in value of the company assets consequent upon its failure.'

Nothing beats the possession of tangible security in small business lending and it is often possible to obtain this after a manager has

Statement of affairs at 9 January 1986

	Book amounts		Estimated to realise/rank
Assets			
Leasehold property improvements		5,334	—
Fixtures and office equipment	3,017		
less: seized by distraint	3,017		—
Plant and equipment	1,439		
less: seized by distraint	1,439		—
Motor van	1,132		
less: seized by distraint	1,132		—
Trading stocks	14,000		
less: seized by distraint	14,000		—
Trade debtors	61,748		
less: charged to a Financing Co Ltd	28,425	33,323	12,000
VAT–net debtor (estimated)		1,000	1,000
Extended warranty claims		15,000	—
			13,000
Preferential creditors			
Inland Revenue		15,422	
Rates		4,734	20,156
Estimated deficiency – preferential creditors			−7,156
Secured creditors			
A Financing Co Ltd	28,425		
less: contra	28,425		
Company's bankers (debenture)		4,093	4,093
Estimated deficiency – secured creditors			−11,249
Unsecured creditors			
Trade creditors per list		77,088	
Other accrued expenses (estimated)		6,000	
Directors loan account		1,208	
Due to holding company		25,000	109,296
Estimated deficiency – unsecured creditors			−120,545
Share capital			
Issued share capital		60,000	60,000
Estimated deficiency – members			£ −180,545

Notes

1. The figures are subject to costs of liquidation and realisation. They are also subject to the amounts to be proved by creditors.
2. On 20 December 1985 certain assets were seized by agents acting for the company's landlords, in distraint for arrears of rent totalling £7,713.
3. Excluded from unsecured creditors are amounts of £5,985 due to a supplier, as this is subject to litigation and the company's counter claims exceed this amount.
4. Excluded from unsecured creditors are amounts of £17,500 approximately (the liability is in Danish Kroner) due to a Danish company. This amount is disputed and is the subject of High Court action. The company's counter claim is for damages as well as the honouring of an extended warranty claim for the service, repair and modification of its products. It is thought unlikely that the liquidator will have the financial resources from the realisation of assets in order to pursue these claims to a satisfactory resolution of the litigation.
5. Assets which were used by the company as lessee and which were owned by leasing companies have been excluded from the statement of affairs as the estimated sale proceeds of the assets appears in all cases to be less than or equal to settlement liabilities.

Fig. 7.3 The Statement of Affairs of a limited company, with notes relating to its winding-up

declined an initial proposition on the ground of insufficient security being offered. It is only to be expected that customers will look after their own situation and if there is a chance that they can negotiate an overdraft without security or with weak security they will take it. It is therefore the manager's responsibility to stick to the terms on which the bank is prepared to make an advance available. Such implacability can often force the customer to offer further security if it is available.

ENGAGEMENTS, INDEMNITIES AND BONDS

Managers will often be asked to enter into engagements whereby the bank is bound to make payments in the event of proper demand being made upon them. Requests for the bank to enter into such contingent liabilities need to be assessed in the same way as a request for an advance. The effect that such payment by the bank will have on the customer's finances must be assessed. Usually, the amounts involved with private customers in this area are small and give rise to few problems. However, in the case of limited companies the amounts can run into millions of pounds, e.g. where bonds are given in respect of export contracts.

There are certain contingent liabilities of this nature which can be virtually ignored in so far as risk is concerned, e.g. an indemnity in respect of a lost share certificate. On the other hand, where amounts of any real size are involved then that sum should be aggregated with the customer's other borrowing facilities and the overall total recognised as being a real risk to the bank, with an assessment being made on that basis. In these situations managers should remember that with many engagements, indemnities and bonds, the bank will be required to pay upon first demand from the person to whom the engagement is given. These demands may come direct to the branch or via its head office. In the former case the manager should discuss the demands with the lending controller, even though this will not change the fact that the bank will have to meet its responsibilities on the day the demand is received or immediately after and will have to debit the customer's account accordingly. The customer will, of course, be informed of the situation by telephone but it is very unlikely that anything the customer can say will enable the bank to avoid its commitment. The commitment is a direct contract between the bank and the person to whom the engagement has been given.

Before entering into such a situation the manager should ensure that the customer realises that demand will lead to instant payment by the bank and that the customer will have to deal with the resulting situation as best he can.

OTHER SECURITIES

There are sundry other assets that can be offered to secure an advance, for instance, commodities, mortgages of ships and aircraft, assignments of debts and interests in trusts. Advances against these other types of security are relatively rare and a manager can pass his entire career without encountering them once. They should be regarded as being of a special nature and on the first occasion the matter arises a manager would be well advised to seek advice from head office and perhaps visit a manager with experience in the relevant area before proceeding. From the practical standpoint, it is not worth contemplating an advance which is to be secured by pledge over goods unless the customer is very well known, financially strong and known to be trustworthy in business transactions. Considerable trust will be invested in such a customer to ensure satisfactory repayment against goods and his standing is therefore of major importance.

COMPLETION OF FORMS OF CHARGE

The preparation and completion of forms of charge is a routine procedure which can often be left to the attention of security clerks. Having been completed, these forms will be placed with the securities to which they pertain in the branch strong-room and they remain there untouched for years pending repayment of the advance. However, at the first signs of a customer appearing to be in difficulties the manager must inspect the security to ensure that it is in order. If at that point forms of charges are found to have been incorrectly completed in any way then the chances of recovering an advance through the security will be in jeopardy. This situation would certainly put a manager in an embarrassing position when writing his report to head office.

It is therefore essential that before forms of charge are finally placed in the strong-room a thorough inspection takes place by the manager or a senior official to ensure that the lending is covered. It is not all that rare to find that this is not the case and that the wrong type of form may have been prepared and signed by the customer, that the wrong amount may have been inserted on a guarantee or perhaps that only one party has signed the form where two signatures are required on the document and that the liability of all parties is consequently invalid. Managers should remember that under the pressure of a day's business clerks can make mistakes. Securities are often put away in the strong-room towards the end of the day when staff are hurrying to finish their work. It is essential to realise that forms of charge may be inaccurately completed and a final check must take place.

CONTROL OF SECURITIES DEPOSITED

Securities, including the form of charge, should rarely leave the bank's possession once they have been deposited. If the customer wishes to have access to them then they should be inspected on the branch premises under the supervision of a member of the staff. There might, for example, be an occasion when deeds need to be delivered to solicitors. The bank must only release them against an undertaking not to part with them or effect any change in title and that they will be returned in due course. However, in the case of forms of charge it is best to retain the original document and to send only a photostat copy to the solicitor.

SECURITY AGAINST BRIDGING LOANS

In the case of bridging loans which are based on simultaneous exchange of contracts, there is no need to take a form of charge over the property being sold. Quite apart from the fact that there may well not be enough time to complete such a document, it is not necessary to have a form of charge if the solicitor acting for the bank customer gives an undertaking to hold the deeds to the order of the bank and to account to the bank for the net proceeds of sale. This undertaking constitutes the source of repayment of the advance and can be entirely relied upon. The security as such will be the customer's authority to his solicitor instructing him to pay the net proceeds of sale to the bank for the credit of his account. Once such an authority is in a solicitor's hands and an undertaking based upon it has been given, it is standard practice to regard the instructions as irrevocable unless the bank agrees to dispense with the undertaking. Where a bridging loan is open-ended, it may well be in the bank's interest to take a charge over the property to be sold. This will involve the standard procedure of a valuation and checking of the title.

EQUITABLE AND LEGAL CHARGES

As was seen in respect of stocks and shares, it is possible to obtain an equitable or a legal charge over assets deposited as security for an advance. Apart from the aspects discussed under stocks and shares in this chapter, the bank manager will be well advised to resist any requests for an equitable charge. It does not make sense for a bank to place itself in a position where it could possibly be affected by a prior equitable charge if there is no need to do so. It follows that deeds deposited in security without written charge are not good security. If they are to be relied upon then a legal mortgage will need to be taken.

THIRD PARTY CHARGES

Charges given by third parties should be executed in much the same way as that described earlier on under 'Execution of guarantees'. The point to emphasise is that the manager will not wish to encounter any difficulties with the security after the money has been lent. Nor will he want to leave any unplugged gaps which could lead to the bank being taken advantage of by a depositor in the event of the bank having to realise the security. When the negotiations for an advance are taking place customers will be at their most co-operative and the depositor of the third party security will also be at the point when he is most willing to assist. It is, therefore, at this point that precautions must be taken to ensure that there will not be problems later on.

DURESS, FORCE OR FEAR

If the manager suspects that any duress, force or fear is being exercised over the depositor of security at the time of the negotiations (e.g. blackmail or physical or psychological threats, etc.) then he must decline to offer the advance. The bank must not be involved in any transactions where there are such elements at play because if the security does ultimately have to be realised, it may be possible for the depositor to plead duress and to allege that the manager was aware of it. This could upset the bank's rights over its security.

By the same token, the bank itself must not apply duress in any manner in order to coerce a customer into giving security. This might occur in situations where the bank is looking for additional security in order to cover borrowings permitted in excess of the current security cover. In order to avoid any such conflict with legal requirements, it is better to insist that the customer executes any form of charge in the presence of a solicitor. The latter should be requested to explain the document and the effect of the transaction. Having ensured that the solicitor was present as a witness to the customer's signature, the bank manager can say that the customer was independently advised and had been given the opportunity to refuse to execute the form of charge had he or she wished to do so.

SUMMARY

Apart from cases where formal lending schemes are used when a head office has decided to dispense with the necessity of security, it should by now be evident that there are considerable dangers in unsecured lending to anyone other than a small number of very creditworthy customers. The taking of security ought to ensure that a bank stays in charge of any particular lending situation and that control is not permitted to pass into the hands of customers. Where sound security exists a manager has a safeguard which will ensure ultimate repayment of the loan and which will save the bank from being exposed to unnecessary risks.

CHAPTER 8

Bad and doubtful debts

'Anyone can hold the helm when the sea is calm'
Maxims, No. 108, Publius Syrus, 1st Cent. BC

However competent a manager is in his lending practice there is no doubt that from time to time a bad debt will arise or the repayment of an advance will become doubtful. Most bad debts pass through the doubtful stage prior to a real loss of money occurring and there are a host of reasons for lending becoming unsatisfactory: customers not being able to manage their businesses efficiently, a principal member of the company dying, a falling demand for goods or services, excessive drawing by the proprietors of the business or failure to live within their means and even adverse weather conditions working against a particular business.

In general, banks tend to support an ailing business account longer than is desirable in an effort to be entirely fair to a customer's trading position. A bank may do this rather than acting in a peremptory manner and cutting off a supply of credit at an early stage when it may actually be more advantageous to the bank to do so. For public relation reasons banks will not wish to be seen to be acting in a draconian manner. The branch manager must learn the skill of preventing the worst possible situation occurring whilst also allowing the customers every reasonable chance to get out of their difficulties. In order to do so he must learn to recognise early signs of a potential bad debt.

INDICATIONS OF EMERGING BAD DEBTS

The current account is usually the first barometer to indicate that all is not well with an account – excesses over limits may appear; there may be an absence of money to meet cheques; special presentations of the customer's cheques will be made where it has not been normal practice or the swing on an overdraft from debit to credit may deteriorate so that the balance is permanently in debit, with the minimum amount borrowed increasing steadily month by month. In cases where no borrowing facilities exist a warning sign will be the sudden appearance of unauthorised overdrafts. The need for the bank to return cheques or even to consider the return of cheques is also an obvious pointer to a poor situation. Once an element of doubt comes into a manager's mind then he must act. Delaying in the hope that things will sort themselves out without his intervention may well disadvantage both bank and customer. Unless the manager makes a point of speaking plainly with the customer at this point matters will probably deteriorate further.

Information

The manager must ensure that he is in receipt of reliable information about a private customer's affairs or the trading position of a business, including in the latter instance an up-to-date set of figures showing debtors, creditors, stock, etc. Customers must be made to understand that the bank will start to call in an advance if such information is not produced swiftly. If the manager feels he cannot rely upon the accuracy of the information supplied by a customer he should instruct the auditor (if there is one) about the bank's requirements, stressing the need for urgency and giving a date by which the information must be presented.

In cases where the company employs a chartered accountant (or an unqualified accounts manager) the bank manager should insist on having a private discussion with that individual. This would not be an unreasonable request where doubt exists over the viability of continuing the advance. If customers resist such an interview it is probable that they have something to hide. In some cases the directors of the business may even have ignored their accountant's advice on certain courses of action. The business may consequently be in trouble and the directors will be trying to hide the fact that they failed to heed their employee's advice. Such employees can probably give the manager information which will help him to take a firm decision one way or another and they may also be the people who have to implement any recovery programme.

HELPING THE CUSTOMER TO FACE FACTS

The manager's lending controller will need to be informed of any particularly critical situations and he will obviously be willing to offer advice. In fact the controller must always be consulted if further funds are to be put into an ailing business. However, having established what the bank's view is, it is up to the manager to initiate the discussions with the customer, to obtain all the relevant information and to form his own opinion as to the likelihood of a doubtful debt deteriorating or recovering.

In dealing with companies and partnerships the manager often communicates solely with the director or partner who looks after negotiations with the bank. However, there will be times when the manager recognises that a board or partnership is divided on policy that one or more directors or partners are not pulling their weight or that there is a serious degree of animosity between all concerned. If at the same time repayment of an advance begins to look doubtful, he should insist on a meeting with all the directors or partners. At such a meeting he should outline his fears for the future of his advance and the implications for the business if internal problems are not resolved. If the manager's presentation is convincing it can be very effective in checking decline, particularly if the livelihood of those involved is dependent upon the business. Some of those attending the meeting may have previously been quite unaware of the danger facing the business. Equally, the manager will probably be better informed about future prospects after the meeting has taken place. Often a bank manager is able to exercise an objectivity the customers in question lack. For example, people may be investing personal money into a family business to keep it going when all real hope of its survival has gone. It would have been far better to have wound-up the business rather than waste further money.

A manager must recognise that running a successful business is a precarious venture and that from time to time he will deal with accounts where there is a downturn in business. What needs to be recognised in these situations is when a down point has become irreversible. Managers need to be one step ahead of their customers and if they are may consequently be aware of what is happening before the customer is prepared to admit to serious difficulties. Having decided that a business is heading for failure, the manager needs to tell the customer of his fears and what is causing them. The customer's reaction may be one of agreement or one of total disbelief. They may refuse to co-operate and start to complain that 'banks take away the umbrella once it starts raining'. However, the manager has a duty to protect his own position as the bank's business is to lend money only to healthy, ongoing customers.

DISCARDING POTENTIAL LOSSES

Having accepted the principle that the bank must protect its interests there is nothing wrong with a manager ridding the bank of an account which is proving unsatisfactory. Once the confidence of the bank in its customer has been lost it is difficult to re-establish. If the manager's decision is made at the most opportune moment there will be some assets left in a business and it will have some sort of short-term trading future. A manager should then insist that the terms of any advance are strictly observed or that the account is conducted strictly in credit. It should be made clear to the customer that the bank is not going to change its view of the situation and that it might be in the customer's best interest to seek finance elsewhere. Such a statement often forces customers to appreciate the severity of their situation.

This is also the natural time to try to get repayment of any borrowing – although it may also be the time when a customer is least able to repay. The customer may decide to apply to another bank for funds and this could relieve the situation as far as the manager of the existing bank is concerned. (The customer may then find that applications for money elsewhere are declined and be forced to recognise the validity of his former bank's decision.) The same sequence of events can occur in both business and private accounts. A manager should not think that there is anything immoral in trying to get rid of an account which he regards as unsatisfactory. If another lender considers that it is a fair business opportunity then it is simply a case of one person's judgement against another's. The manager's duty is to extricate the bank from any position that is likely to lead to a bad debt.

All accounts which fall into this doubtful area call for a balanced professional judgement. Where the problem has been confronted at an early stage and where the customer is willing to collaborate it may well be possible to formulate a policy for the survival of the business. The customer would probably need to supply regular statistical information and the manager could perhaps increase the limit – where he felt that this would not be throwing good money after bad. It may be that by some modification of repayment terms or by the taking of additional security the bank could find a satisfactory recipe for continuing with an advance and for the customer to regain ultimately a sound financial footing. Many personal and business accounts have been rescued in this way. However, it is not always possible to get this degree of co-operation, as, for example, the customer may not recognise that he has a problem or may not have confidence in the manager, or vice versa. Equally, a precarious position may emerge too late for a survival programme to stand any chance of succeeding.

BAD DEBTS

Unless it has been well established that a customer has no assets or source of funds to which to turn, bad debts should be pursued vigorously. The longer a bad or doubtful debt is left the less likelihood there is of eventual recovery. However, the cost of pursuing debts must be weighed against the likelihood of success in obtaining repayment. (For further details see 'Receivers' fees' in Chapter 7.) If a bank appoints a firm of solicitors it should preferably have a debt-collection department. They should be instructed on precisely how far they can proceed without further reference, e.g. to judgment debt but not bankruptcy. It is important to phone them regularly to ensure that they are keeping up the pressure for payment and are moving as quickly as possible in the circumstances. Repayment can often be obtained from reluctant customers when they realise that the bank is prepared to proceed with bankruptcy or liquidation. As a last resort the problem can be handed over to a respectable debt-collection agency.

Where there is no known source of repayment then a bank is forced either to realise any security it has or to appoint receivers or liquidators to rescue what they can from the remains of a company. A bank can also sue for a debt in court. Where there is no security a bank is obviously totally exposed but even where it does exist a bank may only obtain partial repayment. However, a bank is obviously more willing to exercise patience or put in additional funds if the overall position is secured.

Residential property in relation to bad debts

Where security is in the form of property and where that property is the home of the depositor then the manager needs to think hard about the consequences of realising it. He should do this long before the debt becomes bad – indeed even before the money is lent. On many occasions a business needing money can only obtain that money by the proprietors providing their own home as security. If the business fails it is bad enough for customers to lose income and to have all the problems associated with a business collapse without becoming homeless as well. It is therefore especially important when lending in such circumstances for the manager to discuss with the customer the problems that will ensue should such a situation arise and to do everything possible to prevent the bank from having to fall back on that security.

However, many good and useful advances are regularly made to customers for the support of their business where the only security is residential property and where ultimately the business has grown to such a size that the security has been released. This is a good target to aim for as, from the security angle, it is best to have a customer's private life separate from his business life as far as possible.

Fraudulent preference

Section 44 of the Bankruptcy Act 1914 states the following:

> 'Every conveyance or transfer of property, or charge thereon made, every payment made, every obligation incurred and every judicial proceeding taken or suffered by any person unable to pay his debts as they become due from his own money in favour of any creditor, or of any person in trust for any creditor, with a view of giving such creditor, or any surety or guarantor for the debt due to such creditor, a preference over the other creditors, shall if the person making, taking, paying or suffering the same is adjudged bankrupt on a bankruptcy petition presented within six months after the date of making, taking, paying or suffering the same, be deemed fraudulent and void as against the trustee in the bankruptcy.'

Various Companies Acts since 1929 have applied the same rules to limited companies whose debts are deemed to be fraudulent and void against the liquidator.

The object of the enactment is to ensure fairness between creditors where the debtor is on the verge of bankruptcy or liquidation and wishes to pay off one creditor to the disadvantage of others. Nevertheless, it is possible for an alert creditor to press a debtor to reduce or repay the amount owing to him, and any sums received as a result of that pressure do not then come within the terms of the Acts mentioned above and may be retained by the creditor. It has thus been held that fraudulent preference is an act of freewill by the debtor. Therefore, for example, if a bank's advance is unexpectedly repaid by a business in debt then the manager should wonder if the bank has been fraudulently preferred and should make enquiries to this effect. The manager should be especially suspicious if following the repayment he was promptly asked to give up the security. In such a case he might find that a trustee in bankruptcy or a liquidator would eventually apply to the bank for reinstatement equalling the amount of the debt on the grounds that the bank has been fraudulently preferred and the bank would then be left without its security to fall back upon.

The fact that a bank cannot be fraudulently preferred if it has put pressure upon its customers is an important consideration where an advance is doubtful and the bank is seeking repayment. The best policy is to write to the customer asking for reductions and insisting that they be met. Where the security is personal security, e.g. a house or a guarantee, then a manager may well find that by placing pressure on his customer in this manner the indebtedness will be reduced. There is no point in the manager hesitating about the finer details of the situation. It is his responsibility to obtain repayment of the funds lent, and as the saying goes 'the devil take the hindmost'. The hindmost at this stage are likely to be the PAYE, National Insurance and VAT authorities. When bankruptcy or liquidation actually occurs they receive preferential treatment over the bank. There will then be no chance of the bank being paid ahead of preferential creditors, so the time to act is before the latter are established as such.

CLOSING OF ACCOUNTS

Most bank advances are repayable upon demand and that fact must be clearly established with customers when writing to confirm an overdraft or loan limit. This is usually stated in words such as 'The bank is pleased to make available an overdraft limited to £*x* on the usual banking terms, repayable on demand'. The customer should be assured that this power will not be used in an arbitrary manner and that whilst his account is conducted satisfactorily and in accordance with the terms of the advance he has nothing to fear. However, once the terms of advance are broken by the customer and the bank is justifiably concerned about the repayment of the advance, formal demand may be made in writing. This will stop all debit transactions upon the account although credits may be received to reduce the indebtedness. In such circumstances the customer may open an account elsewhere or persuade the bank through fresh proposals to continue to act for him. In the latter situation, a new account should be opened in order to avoid the rule in Clayton's Case and should normally be conducted in credit whilst the old account remains dormant.

If the manager decides to close an account which has a credit balance after the conclusion of unsatisfactory behaviour by the customer, he should advise the customer in writing with a reasonable period of notice. What constitutes a reasonable period will depend upon the individual customer's circumstances, but it will usually be longer for a business account than for a private one. A month is generally considered sufficient but this is a rule of thumb and attention must be given to the individual difficulties a customer will face if asked to close a credit account in this manner.

A situation can develop where the period of notice elapses and the notice to close has been ignored. The generally accepted practice in these circumstances is to refuse to accept any credits and to honour cheques until the balance is exhausted. If funds are received which have been paid in elsewhere, they should be credited to a suspense account. The customer should be advised of this action and asked how the money is to be returned.

SUMMARY

When advances to accounts in the private sector become doubtful a lender often has to rely solely on the information that can be obtained from the borrower regarding the prospects of repayment. Such information may be scanty and unreliable. A lender's response must be firm and forceful and he should remember that diplomacy at the outset may produce better results than threats.

Information about bad debts in the business sector may come from the auditors, from employees of the firm in question, from accounts and business records, as well, of course, as from the proprietor. Vigorous enquiry will often result in an accurate picture of the state of affairs being obtained quite quickly. Immediate action is necessary where there are unfulfilled promises of repayment or obvious strains on working capital. A strong hand is needed at the helm when navigating the stormy waters of bad debt situations!

Having dealt with the important area of relationships with customers in Part II, the next section – Part III – will be given over to describing other aspects of the manager's general responsibilities. To be effective in his job, the manager will need to exercise authority and develop expertise in coping with any situation – whether reviewing the state of repair of his bank's premises or handling competition with other banks..

PART THREE

General branch management

CHAPTER 9

General aspects of branch management

'Haste in any business brings failures'
The Histories of Herodotus, Book VII, Herodotus, 425 BC

It is the non-lending aspect of branch management in which the most fundamental changes are taking place in branch banking today. Advances in electronic technology and the increasing emphasis on the selling of bank services are changing the character of branch life, and the extent to which it will continue altering is difficult to predict. In the midst of these changes there are the customers – who have changed very little in their approach to banks and their needs. (Some electronic devices such as cash dispensers have obviously been welcomed, particularly by younger customers who tend to prefer queuing at a cash dispenser outside the branch rather than coming inside to use either the counter or, where available, the cash dispensers installed inside the building.)

Customers still need the services of experienced, meticulous and caring bank staff. Those in charge of branches will need to see that their staff stay well motivated during times of rapid change, which can be very difficult periods to work through. Bank head offices also need to bear this factor in mind and should try to avoid introducing new systems to staff who may already be feeling insecure as a result of too much uncertainty.

MANAGEMENT OF CURRENT ACCOUNTS

Statute requires that when opening and conducting a current account banks bring themselves within the protection of Section 4 of the Cheques Act 1957 by acting in good faith and without negligence in the collection of cheques – in order to escape being liable for a claim for conversion. It would be rare for the good faith of a banker to be questioned, but negligence in the collection of cheques has been the subject of extensive case law, as has negligence in the opening of accounts.

In order to avoid risks of negligence, the long-established practice has been to obtain two references for a new account holder and then to check that such references are bona fide by reference to their own bankers. This practice obviously slows down the opening of accounts because it is dependent upon the speed with which the referees reply. Where banks follow this practice the manager needs to ensure that there is a good system of record-keeping as the enquiries proceed and that the prospective customer is contacted immediately the bank has satisfactory responses. The manager also needs to be quite certain that the customer has been told the necessary details about opening an account and about when and how to expect receipt of a cheque book.

There are signs that some banks are moving away from this practice of asking for references and are instead relying on a credit agency enquiry on an intending customer. This may perhaps move them outside the protection of the Cheques Act 1957 but it does speed up the formalities in opening an account. For the vast majority of intending customers, the seeking of references is no more than a formality and a bank's overall cost of taking two references in a mass market will be considerable. Banks may consider that the saving achieved by not taking references and the marketing advantage of being able to open accounts more quickly are well worth the risk of sustaining occasional losses from conversion. Whatever the bank's instructions to its manager may be, he will have to delegate the opening of many accounts to fairly junior staff. He must therefore ensure that these staff are well versed in explaining to new customers the benefits of a current account and the manner in which it must be conducted. They must also be trained to detect unwanted applicants. Where there is any trace of suspicion a full investigation needs to be undertaken. For example, middle-aged people who say they have never before had a banking account may warrant further enquiry since they are unlikely to have reached that age without needing an account. University students, however, who call to open an account with their first grant cheques are unlikely to be treated with any other formality than to be told that they are expected to keep their accounts in credit. (The student account market is judged to be so valuable as to outweigh any risks of negligence due to absence of normal references.)

Troublesome current accounts

When new accounts begin to cause problems the manager must ensure that there is a system for referring them to him so that he can close them immediately. Where there is no valid explanation for poor conduct the manager must not hesitate to close the account. Some branches keep far too many troublesome accounts alive solely because they wish to maintain the overall numbers of accounts on file. This is a faulty practice and can only result in a lot of unnecessary work for the branch.

SPECIAL CATEGORIES OF ACCOUNT

Banking customers can be divided into various categories – which include agents, bankrupts, companies, joint accounts, the mentally incapable, partnerships and trust accounts – and some of these categories can be subdivided. As any banking student knows, the law surrounding the banker/customer relationship in respect of these categories is substantial. However, providing that the correct mandate is taken where necessary when the account is opened and that the account is conducted in credit then with most customers there is no reason to anticipate anything other than smooth conduct of their business.

However, there will be times when special situations occur, e.g. the mental capacity of a customer is in doubt or one party to a joint account says that he or she is in dispute with the other, for example through divorce or business. Where there is a stated rift between joint account holders, partners, boards of directors, etc., the manager needs to be careful about the future disposal of balances. Unless the mandate calls for all to sign (as it should with trustees) then the manager should determine the mandate and insist that all parties need to sign future withdrawals from the account until their differences are resolved. The manager must not become involved in a dispute and once the matter is settled should take a new mandate from the parties concerned. Alternatively, he should obtain the signatures of those involved in order to make a final distribution of funds standing to the credit of an account. Failure to take such action can cause repercussions for the bank.

Mental disorder

If there is cause to be concerned about the mental state of a customer it may not be easy to determine the exact situation in cases where a receiver has not been appointed. A bank may therefore be in the awkward position of not knowing whether to continue honouring cheques drawn by the customer and this situation may be temporary or permanent. Furthermore, the customer's next of kin may need to financially support the customer (in hospital for example) and to keep his or her home running. This third party may in some instances need to operate the account without the customer's written authority. The problem that might then arise is that in the event of the customer's recovery or death, the customer or his personal representative may challenge the bank's decision to pay the assets away on the strength of the third party's signature. Therefore each situation when a relative, etc. needs to operate the account will have to be thoroughly investigated to ensure that it is genuine. Once satisfied the bank will then need proof that withdrawals from the account are for necessities by seeing invoices, etc. Naturally, if any doubt remains the manager needs to discuss the position with his lending controller or legal department. When dealing with mental disorder the bank may be willing to pay for necessities through a third party on a temporary basis but it is unreasonable to expect it to continue on this basis for very long. Pressure should be put on the next of kin to have a receiver appointed in cases of lengthy mental incapacity. However, there will be times when both the customer and the bank recognise that the customer's impending health problems are sufficient to require the appointment of someone else to operate the account.

Bankruptcy and winding-up

Cases of bankruptcy and winding-up can also give rise to the sort of problems arising on accounts of customers with mental disorder because a manager will have to determine whether the mandate between the bank and its customer should be terminated. In cases of bankruptcy, rumours are naturally insufficient cause to justify any action. However, once the bank has notice that a bankruptcy petition has been presented against a customer, its authority to pay cheques drawn by the customer is determined. The bank can go on accepting any credits but, as it will be unable to pay the funds away, it should make clear to the customer that any funds accruing to the credit of the account will have to be retained by the bank whilst the petition is outstanding.

Winding-up

When notice of a petition for compulsory liquidation of a company is received by a bank, it is placed in an awkward position because the outcome of the petition may not be known for some time but the company will still be in existence. This is an unsatisfactory situation and it is unlikely that any two banks will deal with it identically. The action taken will almost certainly depend on the bank's knowledge of its customer, the circumstances surrounding the petition to wind-up, and the customer's current needs. There has been an important change in the treatment of accounts in these circumstances (Re Gray's Inn Construction Co. Ltd. 1980). Hitherto, it was thought that banks might get some protection from paying cheques by pleading Section 227 of the Companies' Act 1948, which states 'In a winding-up by the court any disposition of the property of the company . . . made after the commencement of the winding-up, shall, unless the court otherwise orders, be void'.

The key word in this section was 'disposition' because although it had been recognised that the account should be stopped and that the paying of cheques, etc. would be a risk, there was judicial support for essential payments to enable trading companies to continue until the hearing, e.g. the payment of wages. It has also been held that a payment to a company of a credit balance in its own name was not a disposition of the company's assets and that therefore such withdrawals as were agreed should be made in cash. In this way it was hoped to help a company in the period prior to the hearing, in the expectation that the court would find in favour of the bank if a liquidator objected to the withdrawal of funds.

In the case cited it was held that whilst monies paid out in cash to a company were not a disposition, if the funds were put to a use which the court would not have approved, e.g. if cheques had been paid by the bank drawn in favour of the same parties as received the cash, then the bank would not be permitted to let the debits stand. The judgment further indicated that a bank must have complete trust in the integrity and competence of the directors. It must also acquire virtually a complete and continuing knowledge of the affairs of the company (not normally something a bank would do) so as to make a judgement as to the consequences of any proposed action. This knowledge must be sufficient to ensure that any such action was in the interests of the creditors, e.g. they might be better served by closing down the company than by continuing. If not then the bank could not rely on payments made after the presentation of a petition being protected.

As it is unlikely that a bank could often meet with these requirements, then a company's account will usually have to be stopped. An application can be made by the company to the court for an order permitting the bank to continue the account whilst looking for terms that are acceptable to the bank. Whether this can be done quickly enough and formulated adequately for the bank to continue until the date of the hearing is another matter. Thus accounts will normally be stopped once a petition for winding-up has been presented.

Where a petition is for a small sum of money relative to the company's overall free assets, a bank may, if surrounding circumstances warrant, ignore the petition at its own risk and continue the account as normal. Alternatively, the company may pay the relevant funds into court and the bank would thus be sure that if the petition went against its customer, funds would be available to meet the alleged debt.

Undischarged bankrupts

Fortunately, it is only a rare occasion when a manager finds that one of the bank's accounts is being conducted by a customer who was hitherto unknown to be an undischarged bankrupt. Where this occurs the procedure is quite clear. It is covered by Section 47 (2) of the Bankruptcy Act 1914 which says that where a customer is found to be an undischarged bankrupt, a banker must forthwith inform the trustee or the Department of Trade and Industry of the existence of the account, and thereafter not make any payments out of it except under the order of the court or in accordance with the instructions of the trustee, unless by the expiration of one month from giving the information no instructions have been received from the trustee. Naturally, it is necessary to inform the customer of the bank's actions so that the customer knows his cheques will not be honoured if drawn. However, if it is only suspected that a customer may be an undischarged bankrupt, the branch will need to make a search to establish the truth and, of course, should ask the customer to make an appointment with the manager.

Spouses of undischarged bankrupts are occasionally found to be conducting separate accounts. In such cases the bank should establish the purpose of the account and if it in any way relates to continuing a business previously run by the husband or wife, or the manager suspects that there is any infringement of the regulations affecting an undischarged bankrupt, he should ask the latter's trustees in bankruptcy for confirmation that the bank can continue conducting the account. It is not sufficient simply to ask the spouse to close the account when suspicions are aroused.

Executors and administrators

The accounts of executors and administrators give rise to few problems providing the bank has seen the probate or Letters of Administration and has taken the correct mandates. Problems can arise from time to time with claims from third parties upon an estate prior to the grant of these documents. Obviously the will, if it is held in safe custody, should only be given up to the executor(s) once positive identification has been made. Claims in respect of an intestate estate from third parties need careful consideration especially where the estate is small. In such cases the manager may consider it appropriate to distribute the bank balance without Letters of Administration being sought. The bank needs to be certain in these circumstances that those claiming the assets are indisputably the rightful claimants under intestacy law. It is not unknown for one relative to call in the morning claiming the balance on a small estate and another to call in the afternoon making the same claim. It is best for the manager to take his time in these circumstances.

Once a claim has been made the manager should make certain that it is firmly established and should wait a reasonable length of time to see if any other claimant appears. When satisfied, the manager will obviously follow the standard bank procedure for making a distribution of the balance.

Customers trading abroad

Bank services to supply the needs of travellers abroad are simply a matter of routine and need no comment here. However, when dealing with people who are exporters or importers, etc. there is a different set of circumstances and they need skilled handling by the branch. A new manager taking over a branch should quickly discover the level of overseas business conducted at the branch – this will vary from being negligible in one branch to being the dominant activity in another. Needless to say, the manager must acquire some sound knowledge of the banking implications of the various overseas businesses operated by his customers. Furthermore, he must be ready to offer the services of the bank specialists in overseas work whenever the customer is faced with a situation which is beyond the resources of a local branch. It is also important for the manager to ensure that the staff know what they are talking about in these situations and that they do not offer inappropriate solutions to customers' problems.

A particular problem in this area of banking lies in the fact that it is frequently difficult to retain the same staff on overseas work long enough to train them adequately. It probably takes two or three years of active work on overseas business before a clerk is wholly competent, but it is unlikely that staff intent on a career – usually the best quality staff – will be willing to spend such a period on this specialist area. Once trained they might be expected to stay in that role for possibly another three years in order to bring the benefits of their experience to customers. Whether due to career aspirations or otherwise, there is often a high turnover of staff working on overseas business and this can present the manager with a problem. Frequently, the solution to it lies in using people such as older, non career-orientated staff. Overseas work (with the exception of arranging travel facilities) is rarely routine and where there is little demand for such services it is best for customers to speak with the manager himself or his second-in-command.

STANDING ORDERS AND DIRECT DEBITS

Standing orders and direct debits are routine work which has been made much easier through computer systems. Nevertheless, it is work which needs firm control. Where such control is lacking it is probable that the branch has a slack approach to lending control as well. Standing orders and direct debit mandates are accepted on the understanding that funds will be made available by the customer on the due date so that payment can be made without creating an overdraft or taking a balance in excess of its limit. There will always be occasions where funds are not available and so the standing order/direct debit has to be taken out of the day's work. A branch can easily find itself with a pile of unpaid items, with a standing-order clerk looking up the balance of each account daily to see if funds have been provided so that the order can be paid. Confusion can then arise as the clerk will not know whether cheques will be presented against the outstanding balance. Although the bank is in a sound legal position when returning any cheques the overall situation is confused.

There is not the slightest reason for getting into this kind of position as there is a proper procedure which can be applied in such situations. This involves a standard letter being sent when the first standing order payment cannot be made, saying that funds are expected to be provided in advance of the payment, that the payment under consideration has not been paid but that the branch will make the payment provided funds are forthcoming within seven days. Failing that, the customer will be expected to make his payment by cheque and provide funds for the next payment when due. If funds are not available at the time of the next payment then a further routine letter should be sent to the customer, drawing attention to the fact that on the last two occasions funds have not been provided on the due dates, that in these circumstances it is not the practice of the bank to continue to maintain standing order mandates and that as a result the mandate has been cancelled. The customer is then requested to issue his own cheques in future ensuring that funds are available to meet them. Such letters will normally bring a response and the manager can then decide whether the bank wishes to continue the arrangement or not.

Legal position

Managers can draw assurance in taking such action from the judgment in the case of Whitehead *v.* National Westminster Bank Ltd. (1982) where it was suggested that the bank had a duty to pay a standing order on the due date or on the next date when funds were available. The court found otherwise, saying that it was the bank's duty to pay only on the due date (or next business day if the bank was closed on the due date). If funds were insufficient to make a payment on the due date, then there was no further obligation to the customer in respect of that month's payment. This judgment has put banks in a strong position regarding standing orders that are overdue. It is best not to make a practice of inspecting accounts daily to see if funds are available for overdue standing orders as if a customer were to find out about this he could claim that the branch, having established this practice, had failed to carry out its duty properly if receipt of a cheque went unnoticed. Normally accounts that give trouble in this area are also those which are least worthwhile to bank business overall and they can therefore justifiably be closed if the situation becomes sufficiently serious.

STATUS OPINIONS

Status enquiries made by a branch

Status enquiries made by a branch on another branch or bank, e.g. on opening accounts, will be a regular part of branch work, and should cause very few problems. Replies must be passed on to customers immediately they are received. Generally it is considered that when a customer opens an account he has, by implication, authorised the bank to follow its routine practice of responding to status enquiries received from other bankers. A branch should therefore encounter no difficulties in obtaining replies to its status enquiries and these should be made in writing. There are obvious dangers in attempting to reply to enquiries made over the telephone. Some banks have given positive instructions to their branches that no replies will be made in this manner. Where a customer's enquiry is urgent the branch can endeavour to secure an answer over the telephone but it should not be surprised if the request is declined.

Status enquiries made on a branch

As already mentioned there is a good deal of law surrounding the responsibility of a replying bank not to be negligent or fraudulent in its replies. To cite two of the legal precedents, there was the Hedley Byrne case (1960) where it was held that a bank owes a duty of care in answering a credit enquiry. However, it would not be considered liable for lack of care when a reply carried the usual disclaimer of responsibility. Such disclaimers are now at risk of challenge under the Unfair Contract Terms Act (1977). The Hedley Byrne ruling may be upset at some future date by the decision in an Australian case, Commercial Banking Company of Sidney *v.* R H Brown & Co. (1972), where a reply to an enquiry was held to be fraudulent. In an attempt to help his customer through what he believed to be temporary difficulties a manager gave a favourable reply and this was eventually held by the court to be fraudulent in the circumstances.

In practice, bank managers must speak the truth by referring to the facts that are known to them from their relationships with their customers. There is no need to seek evidence beyond a bank's experience and so a reply can be given promptly. Although it is easy enough to give a good or a bad answer to an enquiry where the position is clear-cut, managers must not be tempted into giving an over-favourable reply to an enquiry where they have doubts about a customer's financial position. Providing it is the truth there is no reason why an answer cannot be given to the effect that the bank does not know sufficient about a customer's affairs to speak for the figures mentioned in the enquiry. However, care must be taken to avoid any inference that the customer is not good for the amount in the enquiry – unless that is actually the case.

Where a manager has a business customer in a deteriorating trading situation, he will be aware that any reply indicating that the business is not good or is doubtful for the amount of the enquiry can have an adverse effect on his customer's ability to obtain credit. This is particularly true in cases where one or more favourable replies have already been given previously to the same enquirer. Although the manager is divided between a wish to look after the interests of the customer and the need to respond honestly, he must not lay the bank open to an action for misrepresentation of the true state of affairs. Such a misrepresentation could be considered to have induced the giving of credit resulting in a loss – which would not have occurred had the facts of the situation been made available.

CREDIT CARDS

Credit cards involve branch banks in little work other than the need to answer status enquiries concerning card holders and the paying out of cash over the counter where acceptable credit cards are presented for that purpose.

However, when being asked to advance funds the manager will need to bear in mind the possibility that the customer may have run up indebtedness with a credit card company and that this might adversely affect the customer's ability to repay the intended bank borrowing. When the customer is known to be a card holder it is wise to study the latest statements from the credit card companies. It would certainly be foolish to permit an advance to enable the customer to pay off a credit-card company debt and thereby import the customer's problem into the bank.

INVESTMENT

It is generally acknowledged that a manager cannot, and should not, set himself up as a specialist in investment. However, he should have general knowledge of investment matters sufficient to explain the following: the merits of government securities and other fixed interest securities and the advantages and disadvantages of quoted shares, unit trusts and National Savings investments and the like, including the weaknesses of an investment in the shares of private limited companies.

Where the customer is looking for advice on specific Stock

Exchange investments, the branch needs to obtain a professional opinion from a stockbroker. The broker needs to be told the amount available for investment, the approximate age of the customer and his highest rate for taxation. The reply should be handed verbatim to the customer who is expected to make his own decision from the stockbroker's recommendations. Bank rules are likely to insist that the customer decides himself and that the decision be given to the bank in writing in accordance with normal practice.

However, there will be times when the manager is dealing with customers who are completely untutored in financial matters and who expect a manager to be able to advise them competently on what they should do. It is quite common, having patiently explained in simple terms the pros and cons of an investment, to be faced by a customer saying 'I am afraid I really do not understand these matters but if you think it is all right, I will go along with it'. In such a situation theory and practice divide and the manager, probably relying on a stockbroker's opinion, will see that customer's funds are invested, having first taken a written authority.

It is important to ensure that customers feel comfortable about any investment. If they are the type to lie awake at night worrying about the slightest downward fluctuation in a share, then that investment is not the kind for them, however suitable in theory. Customers' investment needs are also conditioned by any other income they may have, including a state pension. It is a good precaution to ask to see their latest income tax assessment and to know if any other substantial resources and outgoings exist. Banks often have a trustee company specialising in giving investment advice and the manager should remember that he can introduce willing customers to them.

SAFE CUSTODY

The security aspects of safe-custody work were discussed in Chapter 1. A substantial amount of safe-custody work is carried out in most branches and is normally perfectly straightforward. However, on the death of a depositor doubts can arise as to the action that ought to be taken. As death cancels all mandates the estate of the deceased passes into the hands of executor(s) or administrator(s). However, nothing should be delivered to them until the bank has received sight of probate or Letters of Administration, the only exception being where a will is held in safe custody as, obviously, nothing can be done until its contents are known. Usually, one of the next of kin or a solicitor will inform the bank about a death and it is a matter of urgency that the will be opened in their presence to discover who is the executor. The will should then be handed to the executor, after identification, against a receipt. The reading of the will may also be urgent in respect of burial instructions or the donation of the deceased's organs for medical research. Such matters obviously require immediate action following a death in order to happen at all. Where a will appoints more than one executor, the discharge of all of them should be obtained to the safe-custody receipt.

The contents of a deed box may need to be valued for tax purposes, as may any items in sealed envelopes, etc. The preferred procedure is for these items to be opened in the presence of the executor(s), a valuer, if necessary, and a branch official. After the contents have been listed, they can be locked up (or resealed) pending probate or Letters of Administration. If the executor(s), administrator(s) instruct a solicitor to value the contents, this can proceed once the bank is satisfied about his authority.

A similar situation occurs should a customer become bankrupt or mentally incapacitated. In these circumstances nothing held in safe custody should be given up without the consent of the official receiver, or trustee in cases of bankruptcy or an official of the Court of Protection. Where more persons than the affected party are depositors then joint discharges will be necessary.

SUMMARY

Whilst a newly appointed manager is likely to be experienced in general branch management and should normally have little to learn in this area, he will, none the less, be strengthening his grasp of management matters and developing experience simply through holding higher responsibility. His ability to make decisions and act on them in this area will be thoroughly tested and he will thereby acquire the experience which is vital for those aspiring to higher office.

CHAPTER 10

Managing staff

'There is one thing alone that stands the brunt of life throughout its course: a quiet conscience'
Hippolytus, Euripedes, 428 BC

To illustrate the subject of staff relationships we shall consider again the new manager of the Millchester branch of Barretts Bank as he takes up his first managerial appointment. His main goal should be to create a unit that will sell the branch business at the optimum level. (The marketing department of Barretts Bank will use terms such as 'having a good image' or 'customer care' when talking about this.) What the branch manager is concerned with is making sure staff realise that banking is a service industry and that this service should be performed on a friendly, willing basis at all times. There are far too many branch counters where cashiers treat customers with a mixture of indifference and off-handedness and this is usually a sign of bad management. Just as the manager is answerable to his head office for his conduct so branch staff are answerable to him for theirs.

DISCIPLINE

Obviously, one of the prime ingredients of staff relationships is good discipline – that is, discipline applied on appropriate occasions and in a suitable manner. Staff should recognise that they will not get away with behaving in a manner which is prejudicial to the bank's needs without penalty. The manager and second-in-command should always correct lapses in standards at the first opportunity as a lack of discipline leads to inaccuracy, poor morale and an eventual reduction in the overall effectiveness of the branch.

Not everyone finds it easy to deal with staff in a firm manner. However, this is part of the manager's job and he must learn how to do it. After one or two initial problems difficulties should disappear as the staff get to know what is expected of them.

CONCERN FOR STAFF

The manager is not solely a disciplinarian and he must have a genuine concern for the well-being of the branch staff. He should be able to chat about day-to-day personal affairs with them – whether about their weekend activities, their holidays or their problems with the tax man! There may also be times when he feels it necessary to stand up for members of staff who have been unjustly criticised by the personnel department of the bank. When a customer complains about a member of staff in writing the letter should be shown to the person in question so that he may give their own opinion of what occurred. Similarly, if the complaint takes place during an interview in the manager's room, the member of the staff should be called in to give an account of the situation. There is no need for staff to remain in the room until the end of the manager's conversation with the customer, unless it seems to be necessary in that particular situation. The manager must always tell the persons concerned how the position has been resolved.

Branch performance heavily depends on the manager getting staff relations right. For example, 60% of the staff of the Millchester branch will feel that they owe their allegiance to the branch manager, rather than to the bank as a whole. That 60% will be there to do a good, pleasant day's work and will hope to finish at a regular hour. Amongst the other 40% will be career-minded staff who will be looking for a future in the bank beyond the Millchester branch and who will be more interested in the bank's overall activity. The manager can succeed in gaining the allegiance of his staff if he leads them well. He needs to balance discipline with concern for staff welfare and for the creation of a harmonious working atmosphere which will produce the best results for the branch.

HEAD OFFICE INSTRUCTIONS

All branches of Barretts Bank will be subject to head office instructions regarding changes of procedure, etc. Changes are often unpopular and it is up to the manager to support his head office when it is necessary to make them and not to engage in any conversation detrimental to that object. There will be times when he feels that some instructions are ill-advised but it is not his place to pass that opinion on to his staff. If he considers the instructions will have a seriously detrimental effect, what he can sometimes do is to defer taking action until he has spoken to his lending controller or regional manager.

DRESS

It is not uncommon for staff appearance and dress to give rise to problems. The best way to deal with the matter is to consider the expectations bank customers have about staff dress. One doesn't see insurance or sales representatives, air hostesses, shop assistants or people in the professions dressed in jeans or tee shirts whilst at work. Male banking staff should not go around in a suit with the shirt unbuttoned at the neck and with the tie knotted two inches below the neck. Nor should women wear the latest fashions regardless of whether they are suitable for work or not. (There appears now to be a growing tendency towards the provision by banks of uniforms for female counter staff.)

Customers might not have confidence in people too casually dressed and this could adversely affect the branch's level of business. Staff should create an impression of integrity and any who are not prepared to dress in a reasonably neat and conservative style may well be in the wrong job. Any contraventions of suitable standards of dress should be severely reprimanded. It goes without saying that managers themselves should always look extremely well-presented since a smart appearance lends extra authority.

FORM OF ADDRESS

It is a long time since the days when everyone at business was addressed as Mr, Mrs or Miss. Although the current tendency to use Christian names is generally acceptable in the banking world, it is up to the manager to decide where the line should be drawn. There is nothing wrong with retaining for himself the title of Mr when staff address him. Indeed, the majority of customers would look askance if the manager were addressed by his Christian name.

THE SECOND-IN-COMMAND

The relationship of the second-in-command with the rest of the staff is as important to the branch as that of the manager and staff. A manager needs to quickly acquire the respect of his second-in-command as their relationship can be crucial to the smooth running of the branch bank. These deputies have the responsibility of the daily bookkeeping and security of the branch on their shoulders and generally adopt the same standards over discipline and welfare towards staff as the manager.

It is important that the manager keeps his deputy in the picture about everything he does and about everything he agrees as it will be the second-in-command's task to run the branch in the manager's absence. The second-in-command should therefore be taken into the confidence of the manager and his opinion may be sought when the manager is faced with a difficult problem. A manager is unlikely to endear himself to his deputy if he attempts to change office routine without consultation since it is the latter who is responsible for implementing this area of work. Equally, the manager has every right to expect that his second-in-command will keep him fully advised on staff matters.

In many ways the relationship between the manager and his deputy is pivotal to the efficient running of the branch. Occasionally this relationship is poor, perhaps due to inefficiency or to a clash of personalities, and in such cases the manager must confront the situation by discussing it with the person in question. If this fails to improve the situation then the manager will be faced with the unpleasant option of having to ask for the second-in-command to be transferred elsewhere – which may involve the latter's demotion. It is easy to delay such action in the hope that the position will improve or because the manager is concerned about the effect that demotion will have upon the second-in-command and his family. Whatever the reasons, the manager should remember that if the situation has arisen in the first place then probably the deputy's control over the branch staff is also unsatisfactory and may well be causing a lowering of morale. In such cases a large number of people are being adversely affected for the sake of one person's career. Such situations can also adversely affect customer relations.

In such circumstances it is up to the manager to prepare a case for the personnel department, based on a review of the effects of the second-in-command's maladministration on both customers and staff. The second-in-command must be given the opportunity of replying to the allegations, not only to his manager but also to his staff manager (who would be expected to interview the employee in question in any case). Such matters are not normally situations where dismissal is likely to be considered but may involve agreed disciplinary procedures of the bank, upon which the manager will be advised by the personnel department. However, these instances are rare: on the whole managers will enjoy their relationships with their deputies and together they will be able to achieve a smooth-running branch.

STAFF REPORTS

Periodically the manager will need to make a report on each member of the branch staff and such reports should be written in co-operation with the second-in-command. It is helpful if the deputy considers the first drafts of reports and then confers with the manager about the final one that should be produced. Before the report is returned to the personnel department, the staff member concerned should be given an opportunity to read it. Nowadays, in many cases he or she will have to sign the report stating that they have read it.

There will be occasions when the staff do not agree with their report but this should not on the whole sway the manager, unless some previously unknown factor comes to light. This is also an occasion for the manager to indicate how members of staff might improve their performance, and thus their career prospects, and it is vital that managers exercise their responsibility here. Some years ago there was a case of a competent staff member who was in all respects ready for promotion to an appointed position. The only thing working against him was the fact that he had yellow teeth which detracted considerably from his appearance. They were sufficiently bad to make people avoid looking at his face when talking to him. He had probably looked like this throughout his life but no one had ever discussed his appearance with him – presumably because it was thought to be too personal or because those concerned lacked the interest to tackle the subject. Some three years later, by then a frustrated man, the staff member was transferred to another branch where, within a short time, his new manager asked him if he had considered his appearance and whether he realised that the state of his teeth would be off-putting to a customer when discussing affairs across a manager's desk. A dentist soon improved the man's teeth and he was subsequently promoted. This story is a vivid illustration of the importance of using the time of staff reports for frank, helpful discussion with staff about their shortcomings or difficulties.

Capabilities

Staff reports call for the manager to comment on the individual's banking knowledge, their judgement and reliability, their use of initiative and their leadership and co-operation – qualities on which the manager will himself be judged by his superiors. The manager needs to consider how well the individual concerned is holding down his or her present job in the light of these categories and how suited the person is to shouldering extra responsibility. If the manager is recommending someone for greater responsibility then he should ask the person concerned if he wishes to take it on, at the same time taking the opportunity to enquire which direction they wish their career to take. Not everyone wants to become a lending manager – some prefer administrative roles. It is advisable to sort this matter out early in an employee's career so that the bank does not put someone into a fairly senior position who does not really want the post, but who was never given the chance of opting for a preferred career path.

Where a staff report shows there is a serious lack of capability, then the manager will need to invoke the bank's disciplinary procedures, which will involve him in consulting the personnel department at his head office. If the manager is permitted to give a first warning without reference, then he should interview the staff member and state that this interview is a first warning under the relevant legislation, pointing out the exact nature of the deficiencies and the action required by the staff member to remedy them. He should advise the employee in question that the first warning will remain on the records for a specified period, e.g. six months or a year, and that their progress will be monitored periodically (e.g. every three months) and followed by a further discussion. He should end by expressing a hope that the staff member will be able to improve their performance and attain the required level of efficiency. It is important to record the interview in writing, giving a copy to the staff member and obtaining a signature confirming that it has been received. If the matter proceeds to a second warning then an interview is likely to be arranged between the staff member and an official of the bank personnel department, possibly with the manager present. Any further disciplinary action will follow the same course.

Finally, when assessing an individual the manager should remember to look at him in the light of the bank as a whole. A person who is outstanding in one branch may perform only averagely well in another. The manager's job is to report on the individual's capacity to carry out work in any branch of his bank rather than just the one in which they are currently employed.

TRAINING

Staff training is another important managerial responsibility as it can ensure the continuing good performance of the bank and the efficiency of the individual branch in particular. All banks have sound, sophisticated training schemes for various staff levels and a manager should ensure that his staff participate in these courses at the appropriate time. However, there is a considerable amount the manager and the second-in-command can do themselves to impart their knowledge and experience to members of staff as opportunities arise. The attitude that 'it is quicker to do it myself' may be justifiable on occasions but can prevent younger staff from gaining necessary experience. Obviously staff will have to be supervised initially but the longer-term benefits will outweigh any inconvenience or extra work this causes.

Sometimes staff do not understand why they are asked to carry out particular tasks and consequently resent having to do the work involved. This will occur particularly when they don't get to see the end product of the work. A few words of explanation at the outset demonstrating the necessity or importance of the task in hand may well produce a staff member who works more accurately and cheerfully.

Examinations

Where staff are career-minded then they should be encouraged to sit The Institute of Bankers examinations: an Associate of The Institute of Bankers is better equipped to follow a career path than someone who has not studied to obtain a professional qualification. Many banks make the passing of examinations a condition for promotion and this point needs to be made quite clear to all aspiring candidates for executive positions in the bank.

There are plenty of people in banks now aged around forty who refused to tackle examinations when they were young because of other outside interests and who have subsequently much regretted the fact that as a result they were unable to get on the promotion ladder in later life. This is not least because their income potential is limited and this obviously affects their standard of living and that of their family. It is no bad thing to point these situations out to potentially capable young people when they are reluctant to engage in further formal education. If they still resist after that at least the manager will have a clear conscience that he has done all he can to persuade them to obtain a professional status.

SPEECH

The manner in which staff address customers either across the counter or over the telephone may need checking from time to time.

A manager should make a point of telephoning his branch occasionally to see how long it takes for the phone to be answered and to listen to the manner in which he is greeted. Staff should ensure that customers are addressed politely and are not kept waiting an unduly long time on the phone when a query is being dealt with. Persistent rudeness should lead to cashiers being reprimanded and counter-barred for a period in the hope that they will have improved their behaviour upon return at a later date.

STAFF MEETINGS

It is a useful practice to hold staff meetings two or three times a year in order to communicate any points that the bank or the manager thinks the staff should know about and to give an opportunity to air any suggestions or complaints that they wish to make. The first few meetings may well give rise to a number of complaints, some of which will be trivial. Subsequent meetings are likely to be more productive and have a better feeling of staff involvement. The presence of the manager may inhibit younger staff from speaking up so that it may be wise for him to be absent from some meetings and to read the minutes subsequently.

LEVEL OF STAFFING

In clearing banks, the organisation and methods department will normally determine the number of staff necessary to operate a branch's business. This number will naturally be assessed on the tight side to avoid unnecessary salary bills. Whilst understandable this practice can often give rise to an unduly high work load in an expanding branch and the existing staff will have to continue under this burden until they have proved that additional business merits additional support. Once a manager is satisfied that more support is necessary for his level of business, he needs to insist on an increase. Where resources are limited, the manager who prepares a convincing case and stands by it is more likely to get what he wants than those who make complaints about undermanning which are not fully substantiated.

Shortfall in the level of staff

Situations commonly arise in banks where the number of staff employed is not up to the agreed manning level. Staff recruitment in a clearing bank is the responsibility of its head office and the manager of a particular branch who finds himself short of his basic level may be able to do little more than keep complaining until the deficiency is rectified.

During the interim period, branch staff will obviously be taking on additional work which may be onerous, particularly during holiday periods. A manager's overall attention to discipline and care for his staff will reap its benefits at such times. Nevertheless, it is a highly unsatisfactory situation and there is no doubt that banks have often relied heavily on the loyalty (or the lack of organised labour) of their staff in order to achieve economies. This practice cannot be justified particularly from the labour-relations point of view.

Overtime

In the situations cited above it is quite probable that overtime will have to be worked. The majority of staff will accept necessary overtime due to seasonal pressures, etc., but persistent demands for overtime interferes with the social and family life of staff. Where such a situation becomes the norm it is usually a sign of managerial inefficiency.

A manager should normally adopt the attitude that he will not allow overtime and should state that he expects all the staff to be finished at a given hour – 5 o'clock or 5.30 p.m. depending upon the hour at which staff are expected to start work. Once a manager adopts an easy-going view of overtime payments, the pressure is lifted from his second-in-command to see that the daily work is completed on time. Staff hours may then be extended, with a subsequent cost to the bank and the staff's morale. Decisions about when to allow overtime should be made prior to situations in which the question of overtime may arise.

STAFF LOANS AND BORROWING

The conditions under which staff may borrow money from the bank will be clearly laid down by its head office and all members will be guided by these. The manager should be prepared to discuss the financial affairs of his staff where necessary and this may be particularly appropriate when a house mortgage is proposed to ensure that staff members do not make an acquisition which they are unable to afford. Where an employee shows signs of being in difficult financial straits, the manager should immediately discuss the situation with the person to establish the facts of the matter. It may be that a small loan repayable over a few months can resolve a problem. The bank will not wish to have members of its staff in deep financial waters, with heavy outside instalment finance payments or credit card indebtedness. It is particularly unsuitable for banking staff to be in such a position as it may well contravene their terms of employment and jeopardise their career chances, i.e. if they cannot manage their own money it is unlikely they will be able to manage other people's. People working in banks are exposed to obvious temptations if they get into financial difficulties. Happily, occasions of staff trying to defraud the bank are very rare and most staff conduct their finances in a perfectly correct manner.

SUMMARY

The manager's aim is to create a branch unit capable of withstanding pressures and of producing satisfactory service. There will be times when the manager may feel that he lacks support from his superiors but work has to go ahead in spite of this. In such circumstances the manager should aim to attain the same degree of accuracy and reliability as he would under less demanding conditions. Achieving this can be a demanding process as he will also be expected to continue making profits for the bank at the same time. If at the end of his time with a branch a manager has also earned the respect of the staff – respect not popular support – then he can feel satisfied that he has managed well.

CHAPTER 11

Premises

'The beginning is the most important part of the work'
The Republic, Plato, 348 BC

The appearance and suitability of branch premises are the responsibility of the manager and it will not take long for the new manager at the Millchester Branch of Barretts Bank to form an opinion about his own. Obviously the appearance of his premises has a direct effect upon the level of his business: there needs to be adequate square footage and a sufficiently attractive and efficient layout to give customers a good impression and staff a suitable working environment. As Millchester branch has been open for thirty-three years and still ranks as a grade one managerial appointment then it is probably of sufficient size to accommodate the amount of business it deals with. If it is bursting at the seams then the bank obviously has a problem. The solution to it may entail substantial capital expenditure if alternative accommodation has to be found or the existing premises are to be enlarged. Obviously, this would be a long-term project and the new manager should carefully assess its value, having ascertained the amount of consideration that has already been given to the problem by the bank in the past.

MAJOR WORKS

If in the end the bank agrees to go ahead with major changes in the premises or a move into new premises the manager will naturally receive the assistance of the bank's premises department. This department provides architectural advice, obtains estimates from builders whose names may be suggested by the manager, obtains planning permission and generally provides overall supervision. The manager needs to recognise that he will become the 'clerk of works' in his involvement in this aspect of bank life. He and his staff will be operating the branch after the builders have gone away and the premises department has finished its duties.

The manager will need to ensure that what seems suitable to the premises department will also facilitate optimum efficiency in those engaged in running the branch. It is advisable for the manager to have made his own plan as to how the building work should be undertaken prior to the arrival of the architect to inspect the site and premises. In order that the branch's needs are met the manager must ensure that he has adequate opportunity to discuss his ideas with the architect. Considerable attention should be paid to the final details, e.g. the flow of staff and work through the office, ease of operating the counters, access to the counter both from the banking hall and from the staff side where the counter is enclosed, the efficiency with which cash and book trolleys can be moved from the strong-room (or lift) to the counter, etc., storage facilities and the extent to which any future staff increase can be met. It is the manager and staff (with the co-operation of the premises department) who will have to ensure that all the features for operating the business are satisfactorily arranged. There are far too many occasions when bank premises' departments have failed to create an optimum working condition, either due to their own lack of insight or because the branch itself has not given sufficient attention to the problem.

When the work is under way, the manager will need to keep a regular eye on how the builders are proceeding, drawing the attention of the architect to anything which he regards as unsatisfactory. There will normally be occasional site meetings between the architect, the builders and the bank and the manager needs to make certain that the architect is fully aware of any shortcomings in the building work which need attention.

Decorations

When the work is over decoration commences and it is important to the bank's success in attracting business that an attractive, harmonious appearance is achieved. It may be desirable to obtain the services of a colour consultant from one of the major paint and wallpaper manufacturers in order to arrive at a good result. Such services are usually provided free providing the specification calls for the use of the manufacturer's products in the work.

Redecoration

The services of a colour consultant may also be useful when the branch needs redecoration from time to time and on the whole this is usually the only building work that the manager will have to consider.

It is important that the work is carried out with minimum inconvenience to the customers and staff and that security is maintained. The chief inspector's department should be made aware that building work or redecoration is taking place in order to avoid a surprise visit from the inspectors at such a time.

GENERAL APPEARANCE

There is no reason why the general appearance of a branch should be anything other than clean and tidy. Accordingly, the manager should see that the branch cleaner is doing a thorough job and that staff are co-operating by leaving the branch in a reasonable state at the close of business – covers on typewriters, computers, etc., and counters and desks clear enough for the cleaner(s) to do their work properly. Any tendency to untidiness, especially on the counter, must be checked. This is particularly important where there is no rear counter screen and the whole of the banking area can be seen by customers. Obviously, in these circumstances such things as tea cups and outdoor clothing should be kept out of sight.

The exterior of the premises

Apart from attending to the general decoration of the inside of the branch, the manager also needs to keep an eye on the exterior of the building. Windows should obviously be clean and areas covered with stainless steel, night safes and cash dispensers, need checking for grime from traffic and weather and regular maintenance. It only needs a glance to ensure that the illuminated sign is working properly. It is surprising how often the front doors of branches are neglected when other exterior parts of the building are maintained. Obviously the front door requires as much, if not more, maintenance as the rest of the branch.

The manager's room

The appearance and style of this room can to a certain degree reflect the manager's personality and on the whole should be conducive to relaxed conversation. The manager may like to interview across his desk or may prefer to sit with his client around a small coffee table in easy chairs, if space permits. In either case, during the time that a customer is with him the manager's desk should have no papers on it other than those connected with the interview – it does not give a good impression to have a desk laden with other papers. The manager will need to have a suitable notepad available in order to make notes of the salient points as they arise and of the agreement that is reached at the end. These notes will be used to record the interview afterwards in branch records. In the same way a pad should be used for telephone interviews. Any calendars on display in the office should be framed to contribute to the overall impression of neatness.

SECURITY

The security of the branch premises is a prime responsibility for the manager and is mainly dealt with in Chapter 2. Head office will have laid down regulations in this respect and they must be followed. Whilst the day-to-day security can be left in the hands of the second-in-command it is no bad thing for the manager to carry out an occasional spot inspection to see how regulations are being observed. There are prime risk times when the bank needs to be particularly on guard against robbery, e.g. when the branch is being opened to the public in the morning and when it is closed in the afternoon. Complacency can easily develop when staff carry out routine duties and this must be checked.

The branch will have standing orders that should be brought into operation if the branch is attacked or if there is a fire. It is important that the standing orders are circulated regularly to each member of the staff so that they remain familiar with the action that is expected. Similarly, the branch's 'Health and Safety at Work' precautions need circulating. Fire precautions will include arrangements for evacuating the branch in case of a serious fire and it is essential that fire drills are carried out from time to time.

SUMMARY

Generally it is the manager's job to ensure that bank premises represent the branch in its best light. They are an important factor in marketing the bank's services, and it has been shown by the fact that there is often an increase in business following the modernisation of an office. Substantial sums have been spent by banks over the last two decades to bring branches up to a modern standard and the manager needs to ensure that they are maintained – for the benefit of the bank in business terms and for the security of his staff and the assets he is holding for customers.

CHAPTER 12

Marketing

'Business? It is quite simple. It's other people's money'
La Question d'Argent, (Act 2, Sc. 7),
Alexander Dumas the Younger, 1857

Certainly the business of banking is about other people's money – and is in particular about the need to gather deposits from an ever-widening number of customers and to lend that money on a profitable basis to those requiring credit. The situation in which twelve clearing banks had virtually the entire financial market to themselves and could afford to do without a marketing policy has gradually declined since the Second World War. Although in those days attention was given to the total amount of deposits lodged and the total amount of money lent at each branch, together with overheads and commissions, no firm management policy was ever applied to commission income. When, during the late 1960s, banks began to implement policies aimed at a common commission charge to their customers it took a further decade before banks published a 'tariff' for private account customers.

The competition to obtain 'other people's money' is now intense, as is the drive to sell the other services which banks now provide. Fundamental changes have taken place in the 1980s which have resulted in banks establishing separate corporate customer branches or offices with the intention of continuing to provide largely personal account services from their main branch network. As a consequence managers have today had to face considerable change in their working lives: some have been moved into corporate branches or offices and some have been retired early. At the same time the status of the person in charge of the private customer branch has been reduced. With the transfer of business accounts to newly designated corporate branches, less expertise is required to run many branches thus affected. Therefore, the seniority of the person in charge has often been reduced by transfer of staff i.e. there may be no one of managerial status at the branch and it is run by someone of second-in-command seniority.

These changes have arisen through the general acceptance of a marketing policy that stresses the need for greater sophistication in lending to the business community and the need to provide time and resources to the local branch network in order to maximise the benefits in the private customer base – all this being done while providing other banking services. Naturally, the marketing of services suited to businessmen's needs has become the responsibility of the lending manager. The following quote gives some idea of how times have changed: Mr Fred Crawley, Chief General Manager of Lloyds Bank was reported in *Banking World* in May 1985 as saying, 'a branch on a university campus might promote . . . personal loans to a youth market of undergraduates . . .' Such a statement would have been considered outrageous several years ago.

As branch networks are reshaped to meet the needs of different customers, every manager becomes involved in a marketing operation. He will be given targets which he will be expected to achieve and will have to give sound reasons if he fails to meet them.

TARGETS

It is not too difficult for a bank to set the overall targets it wishes to achieve for individual services in any one particular year and to sub-divide them so that each branch receives a share of the overall requirement. Difficulties arise, however, from the very nature of banking business, e.g. branches are limited to the cross-section of the public that banks at their particular branch. Furthermore, as the relationship between the bank and customer is a long-term one the approach needs to be different to that of an industrial/commercial activity where often the target is to make one-off individual sales of an easily identifiable product. Mr Crawley is also reported as saying

> 'There are practical constraints to be recognised in branch marketing plans. They include initial inexperience in the arts of selling, inadequate knowledge of the increasing range of services on offer, scepticism as to the rewards for marketing successes and, perhaps most notably, the branch workload, with its historic and vital accent on the importance of successful lending.'

The new manager at the Millchester Branch of Barretts Bank will have to be aware of these constraints and see that his eleven staff are trained as well as possible to sell bank services. This is a difficult task in the face of the pressures of the daily branch business and staff who are often kept late for training sessions can become generally demotivated. Nevertheless, the manager must use his staff to create his own sales force even though all of them have other duties in addition to selling. He will be engaged in a great deal of organisation of both their time and his own.

MAILSHOTS

One would hope that the mass mailshot which was so much a part of the early days of bank marketing has disappeared for good. Such mailings almost never produced a very good result – a 4% response was regarded as satisfactory – and their drain on limited branch resources was difficult to justify. Furthermore, customers nowadays regard such shots as just more 'junk mail' coming through their letter boxes. It is far better for managers to concentrate on a small segment of their customers which they think would benefit from a particular service and write to them personally, giving as little indication as possible that such a letter is part of a larger marketing exercise. The letter should set out what the benefits of the particular service are to those particular customers. After a few days this should be followed up by a phone call asking whether the customer is interested in the service and suggesting possible future discussions within the branch or at the customer's home. This type of marketing approach is much more likely to succeed with customers, who could be pleasantly surprised at the personal interest shown by the bank even if the particular service offered is not required. Such a conversation will also provide an opportunity to introduce other bank services and to condition customers into approaching the bank when the need arises.

In order to meet branch targets, a marketing programme should be continuous and if, for example, at the Millchester Branch twenty letters were sent out a week (i.e. 1,000 letters per year) then over two years the branch would probably reach nearly every customer worth approaching. The follow-up could be undertaken by the manager, his second-in-command and two other well-trained branch personnel and would involve no more than five phone calls a week – by no means an onerous task. The use of word processors would naturally make such a target easily attainable. Marketing programmes require a realistic approach in order to be achievable. If marketing programmes are based on an *ad hoc* approach of tackling the task in three or four days a month, the likelihood is that staff shortages and holidays, etc. will interfere with it and the whole programme will become haphazard and ineffectual.

TRAINING STAFF AS SALESMEN

The manager must ensure that his staff are adequately prepared to tackle follow-up to mailings, checking that they are conversant with the benefits which customers will derive from the service and that they know precisely what customers need to do once persuaded to accept the service. The manager must ensure that his staff are trained to combat negative replies by asking as politely as possible the customer's reasons for not wishing to participate. Staff may then be able to overcome objections and bring about a sale. Some banks are now sending staff on selling courses to support branch-marketing activity. This kind of instruction is usually essential if any real progress is to be made since staff have not historically been recruited as salesmen and most of them already have a wide range of other duties to undertake.

Staff also need training to cope with marketing queries when face-to-face with customers at the counter. Although, for example, bank personnel can easily help a customer who already wants to open a budget account it is quite another matter to persuade a customer who is not already thinking of opening one to do so. Staff need adequate training in order to initiate such conversations and they also need to be fully aware of the contents of the bank's brochures when discussing services. Customers will not be impressed by someone who constantly refers to leaflets when talking about a new kind of account or particular service.

MARKETING BY PERSONAL CONTACT

Personal contact, whether through a conversation inside or outside the branch, frequently gives rise to opportunities to sell bank services. The manager and his staff must be able to recognise an opportunity when it presents itself and to make a positive offer of assistance. The manager himself in his outside contacts with customers, accountants, solicitors and others should be able to attract business and should let it be known that he would be very happy to meet anybody who could use his bank's services.

Although most of the public do not regard banks as companies needing to expand their business, a competent manager may upstage his competitors if he approaches his work from this standpoint and uses every opportunity to sell his bank to the public. The manager needs to be seen about his 'parish' – it is no good retreating into the shell of his branch. There are normally places in every area where businessmen congregate either at lunch-time or at formal evening functions throughout the year. The manager needs to attend such events so that he becomes well-known to a wide spectrum of businessmen. If he quietly develops his contacts in this way, he will establish a platform from which to obtain current account business, lending opportunities and the promotion of the bank's overall services. Initial contact with potential customers may not give rise to new business immediately nor may subsequent occasions produce foreseeable results. However, it is important to become the 'alternative banker' to as many non-customers as possible, i.e. the manager to whom non-customers will turn in the event of there being dissatisfaction with their existing bank at some future date.

THE SERVICES PROVIDED BY BANK SUBSIDIARIES

The manager should always bear in mind the services provided by bank subsidiaries – e.g. hire purchase, factoring, trust and merchant banking with a view to introducing customers to these services where appropriate. Product knowledge in this area is not expected to be detailed but he must be able to indicate the benefits of a particular service in general terms in order to persuade customers to adopt it. Once the manager has an interested customer he should try and arrange an appointment at the offices of the branch or a subsidiary or at the premises of his customer. He will probably wish to attend in person at the first interview in order to make introductions and will wish to remain generally in touch with negotiations as they proceed. Where a subsidiary supplies funding to one of the bank's customers a note will need to be made of the amount and terms since that can affect the consideration of a customer's overall credit involvement. In fact in all marketing efforts notes need to be kept so that the branch has a running record as a guide to future activities.

SUMMARY

Building Societies, the Trustee Savings Bank and many other forms of financial institutions are now all fighting for deposits and offering services which were previously exclusively the domain of the clearing banks. It is therefore essential that a manager recognises as one of the prime requirements of his job the marketing of the bank's overall services through his branch. Good managers have been front line salesmen for banks for generations and today, with an even greater emphasis on this aspect of banking and with a far greater number of services available, this role has become even more important.

The newly appointed manager of Millchester branch of Barretts Bank first carried out a stock-taking exercise at his branch in various areas (as described) to ensure that the branch was running on the right lines, efficiently and providing a courteous, adequate service. He then concentrated on developing an ability to assess a lending proposition and to control borrowing – both essential to the efficiency of the bank's operation and for the avoidance of bad debts. As shown, it was important for him to get his staff relationships and conduct onto a sound footing and to maintain presentable premises – two important areas in the context of the marketing efforts. Having dealt with all these matters the branch manager will have as good an operational base as he can hope to get. There is every reason to suppose that with the right leadership and endeavour on his part, the manager can now make a proper expansion of the bank's services from such a base. He must present a picture of himself as a businessman looking for business.

Increased business can come not only through existing customers but also by acquiring a banking reputation sufficient to attract non-customers. There is no doubt that in the past banks have placed insufficient emphasis on marketing their services and this may have resulted in a number of managers adopting a narrow approach to their business, content to go no further than accepting the business which walked in through the front door. If he is to survive in modern banking today's manager must take a very different view.

A manager's personal standing in the district, along with the efficiency with which his branch performs, are two out of three things which will really influence his level of business. (The third influence will be that of his bank's overall standing in the eyes of the banking public. This aspect is largely outside his control but the effect of national advertising, media comments and the like will bring business to his door, especially in the opening of new credit current accounts.) It was once possible in some quarters to get away with taking a less than positive approach to branch work but it is important to recognise that such an era is now ended. The days of the non-commercial approach to banking are long past.

CHAPTER 13

The competitive environment

'A good reputation is more valuable than money'
Maxims, No. 358, Publius Syrus, 1st Cent. BC

The last chapter ended by stressing the increasingly competitive nature of banking today and this chapter will be devoted to looking at what branches can do to maintain their share of business in the face of rapid growth by other financial institutions. Building societies, which used to regard banks as nothing more than a source of their deposits, are now actively challenging the role of banks by offering competing services. This has created enormous competition between banks and building societies for the deposits of private account customers. The market is also seeing strong contenders for the public's money in unit trusts, pension funds and similar financial bodies. The branch manager now, more than ever, is dependent upon the esteem in which his bank is held by the banking public. However, his efforts to bring about positive results locally will, of course, be assisted by the bank's national advertising and media campaigns – which can lead to the opening of many new credit current accounts.

STUDENTS

Many young people when opening an account for the first time decide to opt for their parents' choice of bank. However, there will be some who are attracted to the bank with whose image they can most strongly identify and they in turn go on to influence their friends' choice of bank. It is in the interests of any bank to have as many student customers as possible since they represent a long-term investment as students receive an education which can generally lead them to influential jobs with large salaries. Once a student account is opened it is unlikely that the bank will lose its customer unless service is particularly poor. A student is probably going to be a lifetime customer.

It is at the time of the first grant cheque that a bank account is often required and as the cheque is not received until the student actually reaches university then he may choose a bank recommended by the student's union. Banks in university towns have their own methods for attracting business but local managers in the students' home towns can help by trying to arrange for the opening of accounts with students prior to their going up to university. This can obviously only be achieved if the manager is able to discover which of his customers' children are about to start courses of higher education.

PRIVATE ACCOUNT AND BUSINESS ACCOUNT CUSTOMERS

Customers opening new private accounts are often young (usually 18–26) and they frequently lack knowledge of bank procedures and the management of current accounts. It is therefore essential that the manager ensures that a well-rehearsed routine is followed whenever a new customer calls to open a current account. Customers need to be left in no doubt as to how to conduct their current accounts. All banks have plenty of relevant literature on the subject but often verbal advice is also needed. The new customer needs to know when the cheque book will be available – whether it is to be sent or whether it needs calling for, what other services the bank is prepared to offer at the outset and, finally, when it is likely that they will be issued with cheque cards, autobank cards and the like.

In many branches there is a high turnover of accounts and because the opening of accounts is frequent and time-consuming, only the minimum is done in order to open the account. This can leave customers bewildered or, at worst, wondering why they chose this bank at all. The opening of a current account is an important occasion to a customer. The manager must ensure that his staff do not skimp their work in this area and should periodically check to ensure that procedures are in order. New business account customers will almost invariably wish to see the manager (or his second-in-command) and any such interviews should be in private. The full range of services should be offered at this point. On no occasion should business customers in particular leave a branch bank feeling that they have received inadequate attention.

CONVENIENCE

There is no doubt that the convenience of a branch to a customer is of paramount importance – people do not wish to travel further than necessary to do their banking. In urban areas those who work in offices need to be able to get to a branch during the lunch-hour. It is unwise to try to retain an account within a branch when the customer moves away from the district. Most customers will prefer to transfer to a branch in the new location straight away. The result of trying to hang on to an account can be that in time the customer gets to know the manager or a member of staff of another bank and then transfers his account there.

COMPETITION AND BUSINESS ACCOUNTS

Generally, marketing for private account business needs to be done on a mass basis. Due to the vast numbers of private account customers, it is costly in both time and money to make individual approaches to attract new business. However, this is certainly not the case when it comes to business accounts. Managers may expect their more important customers to be regularly approached by other banks, whether they are the local clearing bank, American – or other international – banks, Trustee Savings bank or National Giro. He should not be surprised by attempts to undercut his rates or to offer specialised services at a somewhat cheaper price than those of his own bank.

Two considerations emerge here. Firstly, if the manager's relationship with the customer in question is satisfactory then the latter will probably feel that he is already getting a good service and receiving advice which he respects. The co-operation between a bank and a customer depends on much more than the price of an advance alone. Normally, customers will not wish to disrupt an existing relationship which is satisfactory in order to try out the services of a stranger. The manager/customer relationship will be as strong as the foundations on which it is built. Once again, this is where the practice of professional excellence will pay off.

Secondly, many competitors will not be offering the same services as those of the existing clearing bank. They may only offer funds, and, for example, certain international services, at lower rates. Therefore, where it is known that a customer has received an approach from another bank the manager of the first bank should invite the customer to discuss the terms of the new offer. Occasionally, customers simply wish to move part of their business – e.g. the lending – leaving the old bank with the basic service. At this point the manager of the old bank should take stock of the situation. As well as attempting to dissuade the customer from moving by pointing out the benefits of staying with the old branch, he must also indicate that a higher level of commission might be necessary if the more profitable parts of this connection are removed. Where customers deal on more than one current account at different banks, a lending banker will not neccesarily be able to gauge their position and this is obviously an unsatisfactory situation. Such a position may just have to be accepted where large companies are concerned but for small to medium-sized business and private customers generally, a lending banker is wise to insist on all the banking business being conducted through himself alone to try and avoid a 'split banking' situation.

Where another clearing bank is attempting to obtain business it will obviously be trying to offer an improved service to that of the existing one. There are times when a large branch of a competing bank is able to offer a more specialised service, e.g. international work, to a customer than the small branch where he already has an account. If the latter cannot offer the services required then it should encourage the customer to use another conveniently located branch of bank which can, in the hope that the bank will retain the business. This may sound an obvious course of action but it is not one that is always followed. Where competition is a problem managers need to be aware of all possible options and they should recognise that this may involve passing business to branches other than the one at which an account is domiciled.

ACCOUNTS FROM OTHER BANKS

In Chapter 8 the notion of deliberately losing unsatisfactory accounts to another bank was discussed under 'Discarding potential losses'. By the same token, a manager needs to be cautious when accepting accounts from another bank that he is not taking on a customer which they are more than glad to lose.

When accepting credit accounts from another bank, references must always be taken up and the standing of the referees in these instances is particularly important. The branch may inherit someone else's problems and in such cases they will have to act firmly by dishonouring cheques soon after the account is opened if necessary. Any initial interviews with prospective customers ought to be conducted by experienced staff or the manager himself. During the course of discussions as to why the account is being transferred from another bank, it should be possible to establish whether the customer's reasons for dissatisfaction with the other bank are well founded. If wrongful dishonour of cheques or lack of sympathy to requests for advances are cited as reasons the new bank should ask to see the last six months' statements. A credit assessment interview should then be conducted. On the whole, once again, it is wise to stick to the practice of not lending until the account has been open for six months.

Care also needs to be taken when accounts from a rival bank which require borrowing facilities are offered to a bank manager. The manager should ensure that he discovers the real reason for the account being transferred. A wide range of reasons may be given in these circumstances, such as a personality clash with the manager, failure by the head office of the bank to sanction lending which the branch manager had indicated that he would have agreed to, or a lack of business acumen on the part of the manager. Some people will be more forthright and will say, for example, that their present bank will not agree to lend them £*x* for their business and that they have come to ask for a second opinion.

Although managers may be keen to obtain new business from other banks, they should always remember that the other manager is probably no fool and will have assessed the conduct of the account and other relevant information in his possession before coming to a decision. If he has declined a proposition on the basis of that information then the manager being approached must be completely satisfied that all is well before entering into an agreement. The prospective customer is unlikely to draw attention to the weaker aspects of the proposition and so must be asked probing questions. Obviously the manager should not take an unduly negative view of a prospective customer since if he did he would probably never gain any new business at all! He should also be aware that many transferred accounts need a period of nursing before they will run entirely satisfactorily.

During the negotiations for the transfer of an account from another bank, the manager should again always ask to see the last six months' statements of an intending borrower having first established the existing limit. Details of any existing security will obviously be required. It may be that the customer is trying to ignore the existence of a personal guarantee covering the other bank's advance. In such cases it is up to the manager to insist upon the appropriate security irrespective of what the situation has been elsewhere.

RELATIONSHIPS WITH OTHER LOCAL BANK BRANCHES

There is every reason for bank managers to have good working relationships with their opposite numbers in other banks. They should be able to conduct a friendly relationship whilst maintaining a proper confidential business approach to their branch work. Managers will often be drawn together through the local centre of The Institute of Bankers in their efforts to promote the education of bank staff. In the course of their business they will meet at business functions. Whilst they ought always to operate on a 'no name' basis, their association can be very useful if fraud is being perpetrated, e.g. crossfiring. It is not uncommon for local managers to have the occasional private lunch to discuss banking matters in general.

ACCOUNTS TRANSFERRED FROM BRANCHES OF THE SAME BANK

These accounts, particularly the business kind, should be scrutinised and not taken at face value where borrowing is concerned; it is in the interests of both the new manager and the customer to meet for a discussion at the time of the opening of the account at the new branch. The manager is responsible for the credit control of that account in the same way as all others. The previous manager could have taken a view of some activities on the account which the new manager regards as having been too lenient. An initial discussion between manager and customer will determine how far the new manager is prepared to go towards accommodating his new customer.

SUMMARY

A bank manager may well be instructed under bank marketing policy to obtain new accounts by attracting business from his competitors' customers. The better the branch of a rival bank the harder such a policy will be to implement. It is surprising how little business is lost from well-managed branches. If a manager runs his accounts in a caring manner with plenty of personal attention to the customer, a mutually friendly banker/customer relationship will evolve and will protect the account from the sporadic attacks of competitors.

Where business accounts are concerned managers need to carefully research those accounts they hope to obtain, in order to avoid wasting time which could be more profitably spent in other directions.

CHAPTER 14

Future promotion

'Let a man be sure to drive his business rather than let it drive him. When a man is but once brought to be driven, he becomes a vassal to his affairs; they master him, which should by him be commanded'
Resolves, Owen Felltham, c. 1620

If the new manager of the Millchester Branch of Barretts Bank does well, then he will in due course be promoted. If he follows the standard branch management path, he will from time to time move to larger branches – thus experiencing a greater level of responsibility and having charge of a larger number of staff. A branch with some twenty-three staff and no assistant manager is going to make considerable demands on him and will expose any weaknesses in his managerial armour. There will still only be one manager in such a branch but he will possibly be dealing with twice the amount of business he would have in a small branch such as Millchester and there will consequently be considerable pressure on him. It is at such a time that all his previous training will be called upon: he will need to conduct the very best credit control, staff relationships and marketing policy to see him through.

CONTROL OF THE MEDIUM-SIZED BRANCH

The manager's control problems will be eased by the fact that at this level the second-in-command will have an assistant. This means that the manager ought to be able to delegate some of his work, e.g. passing the personal lending to the second-in-command. The number of interviews per day will need strict control and interviews should not be granted to people without a prior appointment being made. One does not expect to see a doctor or a dentist without an appointment and at this level of management casual interviews (except in an emergency) are not realistic.

A target might be to read the post and dictate until 10 o'clock, to interview until lunch-time and to spend the rest of the day on reports and general branch administration. Inevitably things will not run to schedule – if for no other reason than that the telephone will constantly be ringing. Nevertheless, it is a sound policy to make some sort of plan so that staff can have a general idea as to when the manager will be available for queries. Equally, over a period, customers can be quietly 'trained' to know that the manager would prefer to see them at certain hours of the day. The manager of a medium-sized branch must steer clear of being driven into a corner where he has no flexibility or time to move because he has too many customers to look after at once and no time to organise his administrative work. It is easy to become event-driven in any business and bank management is no exception.

THE LARGE BRANCH

If the manager of a medium-sized branch needs to organise his day thoroughly, then promotion to a large branch will call for even greater attention to this aspect. At such branches the manager will have at least one assistant manager and a second-in-command who will be supported by a number of assistants employed to ensure the smooth daily running of the branch. There is a great increase in responsibility between small and large branches and the bank will expect its manager to become correspondingly professional in his approach as he rises up the ladder.

The assistant manager

An assistant manager will have been appointed to the branch to act as a lending manager, relieving the manager of a significant part of the lending portfolio. As far as possible, the manager should restrict the number of accounts that he personally deals with to a figure well within his capability. It is not an easy matter to pass accounts down to an assistant manager when they have been previously dealt with by the manager. Customers may think that they are being treated as 'second class' citizens.

However, the manager must strike a balance between direct customer contacts and the need for sufficient time for the general management of the branch. As the years pass, the manager will obtain new business which he needs to handle himself. Obviously this makes a lot of demands on his time so if he starts his appointment by dealing with accounts that could be looked after by an assistant then he is already beginning to handle too much himself. How he decides to avoid this will depend upon the composition of the various accounts. He might, for example, find thirty accounts with borrowing in excess of £150,000 that he would decide to handle, leaving the remainder to his assistant manager and the other lending staff.

The assistant manager will therefore have considerable responsibility and will undoubtedly need the guidance of the manager from time to time. The amount of guidance required may depend upon the seniority and experience of the assistant manager when taking up the appointment. If it is a first managerial appointment then the manager can be reasonably sure that for the next twelve to eighteen months he will need to provide regular tuition in both lending and administration procedure. He should make his views on lending policy clear and should explain how he expects the assistant manager to perform his duties. A person taking up their first managerial appointment as an assistant manager has an advantage over those taking up their first managerial appointment in charge of a full branch, as the former can easily refer to the manager in cases of doubt. However, whilst an assistant manager is possibly going to benefit from the wider experience to be gained in a larger branch, the first appointment manager taking over the full management of a small branch will undoubtedly benefit from holding ultimate responsibility.

The assistant manager of the larger branch and the second-in-command have differing duties but may well be regarded as of equal importance in the conduct of branch business. Both are in highly pressurised jobs. In the fulfilment of the lending role alone, it is quite possible that an assistant manager will come to the branch in the morning, interview a number of customers, deal with their business problems with the help of only four or five of his staff and go home in the evening having spent a full day shuttered in his office. The pressure of business can lead to this developing into a habit and it is one that the manager should discourage.

In large branches, the manager can himself fall into the same habit, with the result that the other staff at the branch rarely see the manager or his assistant. This does not create a good branch environment and both need to deliberately set aside a few minutes of each day (where possible) to walk about the branch, to observe what is going on and to keep in touch by chatting with the staff. Sometimes it is difficult to find time for this seemingly minor activity but it is essential to do so in order to achieve a co-ordinated business approach to the work. Although the manager and assistant managers are now dealing with the more rarefied aspects of banking, it is important that they do not forget the personal involvement that was necessary in small branches. It is easy to become divorced from participation in the ordinary run of business and this will be to the disadvantage of overall branch performance.

LARGE BRANCH CONTROL

In smaller branches, the manager will only have the second-in-command reporting to him but in the large branches a number of other personnel will need to speak to him and time must be found for this. He also needs to spend time building such staff into a team so that they can get the staff under them all pulling in the same direction. Just as the small branch manager had to do a stock-taking exercise on arrival, the manager of a large branch will need to know the state of the accounts for which he is assuming responsibility. In fact, the manager of a large branch will oversee many of the same areas as he did when a small branch manager, but he will obviously not have time now to get involved in them to the same degree.

However, with the total bank lending being very much greater than in previous branches the manager will have to ensure that his control in this area is entirely satisfactory. Far more personnel will be involved in lending at this level and the manager must therefore check that everyone from the assistant manager downwards knows, and is following, the procedures established for each eventuality. The customers with whom he will now be dealing will be businessmen of standing whose proposals for advances are likely to be well presented, within their means and reasonably easy to sanction. However, no matter how important the customer the manager must respond to the first familiar signs that all is not well and must step in with requests for explanations.

Problems may also be presented by staff involved in lending decisions. They will be far less experienced than the manager and will not necessarily recognise potential lending difficulties at an early stage. Equally, they may not want to admit that an advance which they have sanctioned is looking sticky and so it may be reported to the manager at too late a stage. The manager, therefore, needs to gain the confidence of his staff so that they will feel able to bring problems to him. He should in any case periodically discuss their areas of responsibility with them, thus giving them regular opportunities to ask for information on any lending problems. Action in respect of old and doubtful borrowing needs weekly attention and a system of credit control needs to be established which will ensure that this is carried out in the most effective way.

The second-in-command

The second-in-command in a large branch will be a senior administrative person, possibly holding managerial rank. He will report directly to the manager and will be responsible for the daily administration of the branch, having to devote a lot of time to personnel matters, amongst other things. The morale and overall performance of the branch will depend on the manner in which this work is carried out, on the person in question's organisational ability and on his attitude to customer care. Again, the relationship between the manager and his deputy needs to be well founded so that both are working on the same lines.

It is important, in this context in particular, for the manager to make constructive criticisms of things which he feels are wrong within the branch. As his daily work will probably prevent him having direct contact with many routine matters the manager may only be aware of a small proportion of errors occurring. He will have to ensure that his deputy is insisting on standards as high as his own and that staff are being disciplined in order to achieve them.

COMPLAINTS

The manager should insist on seeing all letters of complaint which are received at the branch and should then pass these on to the appropriate officer to investigate and report back. He should sign all replies going to customers even if he did not compose them. He should establish a rule that he or his assistant manager must be told about all verbal complaints and, where possible, one of them should interview the customer who has the grievance. It is important that where there is a justifiable complaint customers are not fobbed off with some excuse by a junior member of staff, especially in larger branches where staff conduct is more difficult to monitor.

SUMMARY

The absorbing scope of the work of a senior branch manager could fill a book of its own and this chapter can do no more than point to the general nature of the tasks involved in the position. Although it might appear that the work involved is very similar to that of the smaller branch manager, in fact a much greater level of skill and experience are required at the senior management level than is apparent. On the whole, however, the soundness of the foundations a manager establishes during his years prior to achieving senior office may well be the reason that he is promoted to a seniority beyond that of other colleagues.

CONCLUSION

It has been the object of this book to help ease the newly appointed manager through the transition from his previous role into that of a professional banker by outlining the practical aspects of management with which he will need to be concerned. What is obvious is that a branch manager must have a complete understanding of his function, especially with regard to his relationships with his customers and his understanding of their needs and feelings. Although he will not always have had as much experience of customer contact as he has had of routine work before his new appointment, after the first two years in the position a manager should be able to handle people with assurance. Once the lessons of this book have been learnt and tested, the new branch manager will be able to withstand many of the cross-currents of business life and with growing experience, have complete confidence in his managerial ability.

Index